"Thanks, Michael! Your writing has helped me in the past and you've done it again. Combining solid scholarship with a gracious spirit, In His Image *leads readers into insights about what it means to really be like Jesus."*

BILL HULL, PRESIDENT, T-NET INTERNATIONAL

"In His Image *by Dr. Wilkins is a wonderful book. His warm heart and trained scholarship has given us a refreshing book that will become a staple in the lives of thousands of growing Christians."*

DR. R. KENT HUGHES, PASTOR OF COLLEGE CHURCH, WHEATON, ILLINOIS

Dale & Rhonda,

To two of our dear friends who epitomize what it means to be more like Jesus!

God bless you,

[signature]

2 Cor 3:18

IN HIS IMAGE

REFLECTING CHRIST IN EVERYDAY LIFE

MICHAEL J. WILKINS

NAVPRESS
BRINGING TRUTH TO LIFE
NavPress Publishing Group
P.O. Box 35001, Colorado Springs, Colorado 80935

The Navigators is an international Christian organization. Our mission is to reach, disciple, and equip people to know Christ and to make Him known through successive generations. We envision multitudes of diverse people in the United States and every other nation who have a passionate love for Christ, live a lifestyle of sharing Christ's love, and multiply spiritual laborers among those without Christ.

NavPress is the publishing ministry of The Navigators. NavPress publications help believers learn biblical truth and apply what they learn to their lives and ministries. Our mission is to stimulate spiritual formation among our readers.

Library of Congress Catalog Card Number: 97-20830
ISBN 1-57683-000-4

Cover photo: Mark Stephenson / Westlight Stock Photography
General editor: Dallas Willard
Senior editor: David Hazard

Some of the anecdotal illustrations in this book are true to life and are included with the permission of the persons involved. All other illustrations are composites of real situations, and any resemblance to people living or dead is coincidental.

Wilkins, Michael J.
In His image : reflecting Christ in everyday life / Michael Wilkins.
p. cm.
"Bringing truth to life."
ISBN 1-57683-000-4 (pbk.)
1. Jesus Christ—Example. 2. Christian life. I. Title.
BT304.2.W55 1997
248.4—dc21 97-20830
CIP

Printed in the United States of America

1 2 3 4 5 6 7 8 9 10 11 12 13 14 15 / 99 98 97

CONTENTS

To the three remarkable ladies of my life
—Lynne, Michelle, and Wendy—
with thankfulness for our family and friendship,
and prayer for the continued presence of
Jesus in our lives together.

Preface

This book is about the wonderful opportunity of *change*. It considers the reality of change, growth, progress, and transformation in our personal lives. Why is this important? Because our collective culture says that change is unrealistic. The prevailing attitude asserts that our genetic makeup, our individual experiences, and our social conditioning are such overwhelming influences that we cannot overcome them. Life *is* hard. And some of us have experienced such cruel influences that we may think they have permanently shattered our lives. I do not wish, in any way, to minimize those hard facts of life. But in this book I want to give hope of change.

I have seen this change in my own life and in the lives of many people around me. Over twenty-five years ago I met Jesus. As I began to walk with Him I began to change. My heart, my mind, my emotional life, my habits, my actions, my purpose in life, my relationships—everything began to change. It wasn't anything magical or out of the ordinary. Change occurred as I began to live in the presence of Jesus, as the power of the Spirit engaged my life, as the Word altered my values and my direction, and as the loving help of godly friends encouraged me to walk in the path of Jesus. I understood that this was the way the Christian life was intended to be. It was a very natural, yet supernatural, process of growth that included ups and downs, yet was steadily changing me more and more to become like Jesus.

Most importantly, I believe that this is one of the central messages of the biblical record. For over twenty years I have been engaged in a study of Jesus and His disciples. Jesus came to offer a kind of discipleship never before known in the history of the world. Jesus came to offer new life, His own life. Yes, his followers would still wrestle with sin, they would still struggle with dreadful past experiences, and they would encounter daily difficulties and temptations. But Jesus initiated a kind of discipleship that promised transformation. It was not reserved for the Christian elite or the professional pastor. It was the very essence of the Christian life for all believers.

I now write this book to share with you those two profound, parallel influences. Therefore, this is a very personal book. I will share with you my own experience of the Christian life and the experiences of many I have seen transformed. What you read here are true-to-life stories. I hope you will see that the people I share with you have a realistic understanding of life the way Jesus intended it to be lived. It is practical, connected to everyday life, yet it enables us to live a spiritual, indeed supernatural life, in the midst of our everyday difficulties and routines.

Second, this book is based upon over twenty years of research and writing. It is the third, and perhaps final, book in which I attempt to unfold biblical discipleship. The first book, *The Concept of Disciple in Matthew's Gospel: As Reflected in the Use of the Term* Μαθητής (E.J. Brill, 1988/2d ed. Baker, 1995[1]), was based upon my doctoral studies and was published for scholars. The second book, *Following the Master: A Biblical Theology of Discipleship* (Zondervan, 1992), built on the first and was written for pastors, Christian workers, and students. This third book, *In His Image: Reflecting Christ in Everyday Life*, therefore assumes much of the research and conclusions I have set forth earlier. The reader is encouraged to consult those two earlier books for a rather detailed study of Biblical discipleship. At times there will be some overlap, but this present book strikes out in a fresh direction. Here I attempt to lay out a paradigm that connects everyday Christians with biblical discipleship and spiritual formation. It is written for any Christian who desires to pursue transformation into the image of Christ. This transformation is the goal of the Christian life.

It has been a privilege to share with you my life's passion in this book. It has been deeply personal. I will never meet most of you who read this, but I care deeply about you. I will pray for you to the One who knows your name. I will pray that you come to know freedom in Jesus' Word, love from the Father for others, and the fruit of transformation through the Holy Spirit. This is the joy of being formed in His image.

Acknowledgments

Special thanks go to many people who have influenced the writing of this book. I am sincerely grateful to the members of the three churches in which I learned to exercise pastoral care—Carlsbad (now North Coast) Evangelical Free Church, Cayucos Community Evangelical Free Church, and San Clemente Presbyterian Church. Teaching, counseling, and worshiping together with people who live in the daily activities of life has enabled me to see living proof of the power of God to change lives. You were the first to hear the principles I share in this book, and to you I am indebted for helping me to articulate them for realistic life.

I am grateful to the many people in a variety of camp and conference settings with whom I have interacted. I especially think of Forest Home Christian Conference Center, Hume Lake Christian Camps, and Mount Hermon Christian Conference Center. I have been thrilled to hear that the principles I shared with conferees could be carried down from the "mountain high" to the realities of life.

I must acknowledge my indebtedness to the students, faculty, staff, and administration at Biola University. You have labored under my teaching, you have listened patiently to my passion for following Jesus, and you have walked with me in the process for the past fifteen years. I give specific thanks to my colleague, Dennis Dirks, Dean of Talbot School of Theology, who enabled me to have a sabbatical during the spring semester of 1996 so that I could complete this manuscript.

Several people have read all or parts of the chapters to follow. You have offered many helpful suggestions or comments. I am grateful for your influence, even when I did not always follow your advice! I think especially of Robert Saucy, Gary Stratton, Clint Arnold, Walt Russell, Bruce Narramore, and Lynne Wilkins.

I am grateful to Wendy Wilkins for help in tracking down some invaluable resources. You are a great detective!

I have enjoyed tremendously my association with NavPress in producing this volume. This Spiritual Formation Line promises to have remarkable influence on churches, parachurch organizations, and individual believers for years to come. Several years ago Steve Webb approached me about writing a book, but I was not free to do so. Then when the vision for the present line became a reality, he approached me once again. I am grateful to Steve for capturing me with the vision, and for the others who convinced me of its significance, especially Kent Wilson, Mark Kuyper, Steve Eames, and Paul Santhouse. I also am grateful for my editor, David Hazard, who came on later in the process, but who always lovingly pushed me to write to real readers. I cannot overlook Dallas Willard, the general editor, who understands clearly the relationship of discipleship and spiritual formation. We have enjoyed for many years a shared image of discipleship that brings transformation to the everyday lives of God's people. I appreciate deeply his influence not only in this new line, but also in the church in general.

Finally, but most importantly, I acknowledge the penetrating influence of my wife Lynne and our daughters Michelle and Wendy. You have had more impact on my life, and therefore, this book, than any other living persons. You have loved me and accepted me for who I am, but you have never allowed me to stay the same. You have given me the opportunity to learn and grow, and have given me necessary companionship as we have walked with Jesus in His world. Again, thank you, and to you I dedicate this book.

General Introduction

by Dallas Willard

The Spiritual Formation Line presents discipleship to Jesus Christ as the greatest opportunity individual human beings have in life and the only hope corporate mankind has of solving its insurmountable problems.

It affirms the unity of the present-day Christian with those who walked beside Jesus during His incarnation. To be His disciple then was to be with Him, to learn to be like Him. It was to be His student or apprentice in kingdom living. His disciples heard what He said and observed what He did, then, under His direction, they simply began to say and do the same things. They did so imperfectly but progressively. As He taught: "Everyone who is fully trained will be like his teacher" (Luke 6:40).

Today it is the same, except now it is the resurrected Lord who walks throughout the world. He invites us to place our confidence in Him. Those who rely on Him believe that He knows how to live and will pour His life into us as we "take His yoke . . . and learn from Him, for He is gentle and humble in heart" (Matthew 11:29, emphasis added). To take His yoke means joining Him in His work, making our work His work. To trust Him is to understand that total immersion in what He is doing with our life is the best thing that could ever happen to us.

To "learn from Him" in this total-life immersion is how we "seek first his kingdom and his righteousness" (Matthew 6:33). The outcome is that we increasingly are able to do all things, speaking or acting, as if Christ were doing them (Colossians 3:17). As apprentices of Christ we are not learning how to do some special religious activity, but how to live every moment of our lives from the reality of God's kingdom. I am learning how to live my actual life as Jesus would if He were me.

If I am a plumber, clerk, bank manager, homemaker, elected official, senior citizen, or migrant worker, I am in "full-time" Christian service no less than someone who earns his or her living in a specifically religious role. Jesus stands beside me and teaches me in all I do to live in God's world. He shows me how, in every circumstance, to reside in His word and thus be a genuine apprentice of His—His disciple indeed. This enables me to find the reality of God's world everywhere I may be, and thereby to escape from enslavement to sin and evil (John 8:31-32). We become able to do what we know to be good and right, even when it is humanly impossible. Our lives and words become constant testimony of the reality of God.

A plumber facing a difficult plumbing job must know how to integrate it into the kingdom of God as much as someone attempting to win another to Christ or preparing a lesson for a congregation. Until we are clear on this, we will have missed Jesus' connection between life and God and will automatically exclude most of our everyday lives from the domain of faith and discipleship. Jesus lived most of His life on earth as a blue-collar worker, someone we might describe today as an "independent contractor." In His vocation He practiced everything He later taught about life in the kingdom.

The "words" of Jesus I primarily reside in are those recorded in the New Testament Gospels. In His presence, I learn the goodness of His instructions and how to carry them out. It is not a matter of meriting life from above, but of receiving that life concretely in my circumstances. Grace, we must learn, is opposed to earning, not to effort.

For example, I move away from using derogatory language against others, calling them twits, jerks, or idiots (Matthew 5:22), and increasingly mesh with the respect and endearment for persons that naturally flows from God's way. This in turn transforms all of my dealings with others into tenderness and makes the usual coldness and brutality of human relations, which lays a natural foundation for abuse and murder, simply unthinkable.

Of course, the "learning of Him" is meant to occur in the context of His people. They are the ones He commissioned to make disciples, surround them in the reality of the triune name, and teach to do "everything I have commanded you" (Matthew 28:20). But the disciples we make are His disciples, never ours. We are His apprentices along with them. If we are a little farther along the way, we can only echo the apostle Paul: "Follow my example, as I follow the example of Christ" (1 Corinthians 11:1).

It is a primary task of Christian ministry today, and of those who write for this line of books, to reestablish Christ as a living teacher in the midst of His people. He has been removed by various historical developments: assigned the role of mere sacrifice for sin or social prophet and martyr. But where there is no teacher, there can be no students or disciples.

If we cannot be His students, we have no way to learn to exist always and everywhere within the riches and power of His word. We can only flounder along as if we were on our own so far as the actual details of our lives are concerned. That is where multitudes of well-meaning believers find themselves today. But it is not the intent of Him who says, "Come to me . . . and you will find rest for your souls" (Matthew 11:28-29).

Each book in this line is designed to contribute to this renewed vision of Christian spiritual formation and to illuminate what apprenticeship to Jesus Christ means within all the specific dimensions of human existence. The mission of these books is to form the whole person so that the nature of Christ becomes the natural expression of our souls, bodies, and spirits throughout our daily lives.

Reflecting Christ

by David Hazard

Whenever anyone turns to the Lord, the veil [that covers our soul and keeps us from perceiving God in His goodness, love, righteousness, and eternal glory] is taken away—And we, who with unveiled faces all reflect the Lord's glory, are being transformed into his likeness (2 Corinthians 3:16, 18, NIV).

Paul and the other apostles tell us that the glory of God came to live in an "earthen vessel"—and for some 33 years He was, like us, human. In Jesus, humanity and divinity intermingled and were poured out in the most powerful and fulfilling life possible, to the honor of God.

Today, we're tempted to think that *of course* Jesus could live a God-honoring life. After all, He was God-in-the-flesh. Even if we accept Him as Savior, the possibility of becoming very much like Him seems remote, or just too frustrating. Maybe a bit egotistical and warped. We like to insist we're made of lesser stuff—of blood and bone, urges and personal dreams. What would God want with any of this human stuff? Could He possibly do anything to transform us—mixture of high ideals and painful, disappointing realities that we are?

The men and women who have followed Christ through the ages learned to give up making apologies and excuses for their humanity. They did not exempt themselves from spiritual growth and challenge because they'd suffered degradation, abuse and rejection. These are twentieth-century dodges, for the most part. From the earliest days of the church the apostles taught, and everyday Christians expected, that they could be fully human *and* be transformed from the inside-out into the spiritual likeness of Jesus Christ. They learned how to surrender their innermost drives, emotions and ambitions to the life-giving, life-changing power of God. They learned how to pray and work in cooperation with God as new life from above moved from the core of their being, into their attitudes, words, reactions, everyday work, relationships and every activity of life until, in time, they were changed.

What did they know, these Christians who wanted to grow as disciples of Jesus, reflecting His likeness in everyday life? How can we grow and change in spirit today?

These are the questions that Michael Wilkins explores in these pages. Not merely suggesting that spiritual transformation is the goal; not berating us for the slowness of our growth—but giving us sensible help in looking clearly at our lives, and practical guidance to begin cooperating with God's Spirit as He promotes change in us.

Spiritual transformation into the likeness of Christ is not only possible, it is God's promise to every Christian disciple. For this reason, NavPress is pleased to include *In His Image: Reflecting Christ in Everyday Life* in our Spiritual Formation Line.

David Hazard
Editor
Spiritual Formation Line

■ PART ONE ■

IS IT REALLY POSSIBLE TO BECOME LIKE JESUS?

■

CHAPTER ONE

Becoming Like Jesus

Whosoever would fully and feelingly understand the words of Christ, must endeavor to conform his life wholly to the life of Christ.

Thomas à Kempis,
The Imitation of Christ (circa A.D. 1427)[1]

■

Steve and Jill are a model couple at their church. Steve is active in the men's movement, regularly inviting friends and neighbors from the community to his small group Bible study and to the annual gathering of men for the large city-wide rally. Jill is a lay leader in the children's program, teaching Sunday school, helping out with vacation Bible school, and directing the children's Christmas program.

But at home Jill is frustrated and angry, and Steve is increasingly despondent and helpless. Steve is a construction contractor who is good at his trade, but he is a poor businessman. Because he wants to have a good "witness" on the job—as he understands what it means to witness—he regularly underbids projects because he thinks that being a Christian obligates him to be a "nice guy." Over the last 15 years he has gone into debt so badly that he has lost his home, he has had to declare bankruptcy, and he owes the IRS over $50,000 in back taxes.

Jill is tired of making excuses for Steve. She is frustrated at their lifestyle and embarrassed by the endless phone calls from bill collectors and threats of lawsuits from dissatisfied customers. Steve removes himself more and more from church life because it seems impossible to be a sincere Christian and an honest businessman.

Steve and Jill are at the point of giving up. They're almost ready to give up on each other; they have disappointed each other so much that they don't trust each other anymore. And they're almost ready to give up on any progress in their Christian lives. They have heard countless sermons on the "abundant life" and how they should look to Jesus as the example for their lives. But they cannot seem to put together a real life in this hard world with Jesus' challenging promises of abundant spiritual life and radical discipleship.

Is it possible for Steve and Jill to reverse this downward spiral? Is it possible for them to overcome their difficulties and become like Jesus? Perhaps they misunderstand what it means to become like Jesus—that such a thing can be done.

Is it Possible to Become Like Jesus?

I believe that it *is* possible for each one of us to change and grow and to become like Jesus. The central message of the Bible is that sinful, self-centered men and women can be transformed into sons and daughters of God. I have experienced something of this life-change, and I have seen it in the lives of my friends and family, my students, and those in churches I have pastored. It is the message that Jesus came to earth to bring, and it is the message and experience of the early church.

Now *committing* yourself to a life of spiritual change and growth is another matter. I know that there are hundreds of books on discipleship. But perhaps we need a different view of discipleship. I want to help you understand your relationship to Jesus as His disciple in the same way that it was heard by His first followers two thousand years ago. You won't be able to follow Him around the countryside of Palestine, but you will be able to hear His message, look at His life, and allow Him to transform your life so that you are more like Him each day. That is the message that Steve and Jill need to hear.

In a general sense, disciples of any sort become like their master or teacher. Jesus reiterated a general principle of discipleship when He stated that a disciple, when fully trained, will be like the teacher (Luke 6:40). Ancient and modern literature is replete with stories of disciples who would sometimes go to the most extreme lengths to be like their leader.

One amusing story from ancient Judaism tells of an esteemed rabbi who walked with his feet pointed outward, looking like an ungainly duck. His disciples were so intent upon becoming like the rabbi in all ways that they even imitated his walk, following him around the countryside in a line like little ducklings!

But tragic accounts can be found as well. In our day the followers of Jim Jones, David Koresh, and Marshall Herff Applewhite were so entranced that they followed the example of their leader even to death by suicide. Followers of influential leaders naturally assume not only what they think, but also many of their characteristics, values, and goals.

The Goal of the Christian Life

One of the revolutionary truths about the Christian life is that we can be like Jesus in a way that no other disciples can be like their master. In fact, becoming like Jesus is the overarching goal of the entire Christian life. The apostle Paul declares, "And we, who with unveiled faces all reflect the Lord's glory, are being transformed into his likeness with ever-increasing glory" (2 Corinthians 3:18). This transformation is a process that begins now and is concluded in eternal life. Paul elsewhere confirmed that the ultimate goal for those God called is to be "conformed to the image of his Son" (Romans 8:29). Paul proclaims the goal of our growth in new life as a slow change "until Christ is formed in you" (Galatians 4:19). We will hear this refrain sound time and again from the New Testament authors.

Do we really believe this transformation is possible? It sounds too good to be true. Or too impossible. Isn't becoming like Jesus reserved for pastors or missionaries and the like? Many of us labor under misconceptions that keep us from entering the life that leads to spiritual abundance, freedom, and change.

When will I be good enough? For some of us, it's our *perfectionism* that actually gets in the way of spiritual growth. One incident early in my Christian life illustrated this to me clearly. I had been asked to give an account of my conversion at a Christian servicemen's center in southern California. Shortly after I arrived, my attention was drawn to a young sailor who was being counseled by a staff person. He looked agitated and desperate, as his voice broke: "When will I be one of Jesus' disciples? What else will I have to do? When will I be *good enough*?"

I later discovered that this young man was one of the most

committed Christians at the center. But he labored under a load of perfectionism that was crushing his spirit. That is a load that many of us also struggle under. But there are other loads as well.

I don't see that being a Christian makes any difference. Each fall I teach a college course in which I do a survey of the life of Jesus Christ. Part of my purpose is to get my students to understand clearly the impact that Jesus made on the lives of His earliest followers and how that same impact can be experienced in our lives today. A few weeks into the semester one of my students, a girl I will call Kendra, made an appointment to talk with me. Kendra was a very bright young lady. She was an accomplished artist, and came from a Christian home in the Pacific northwest. Then she got right down to the reason for coming to see me.

"You talk about being a Christian as such a wonderful thing. Why should I want to be a Christian?" she asked.

At first, I was somewhat taken aback, since this was coming from a senior at a Christian university. But Kendra came to see me several more times and as her story unfolded, I understood her confusion.

Kendra was born into a Christian home, but her father died when she was eight. Her mother remarried, and her stepfather was the pastor of a local church. The young lady resented her stepfather, and she was unusually rebellious toward him and her mom. She described herself as "acting hatefully" toward them both.

During her junior high school years, Kendra went to a Christian summer camp that broke through to her heart. She got "turned on to the Lord," which resulted in her being convicted about her rebelliousness toward her parents. When she got home she sat down with her parents and apologized for the way that she had treated them. In particular, she told her stepfather that she was sorry that she had treated him so terribly. Since he was a pastor and knew so much about the Bible and the Christian life, she asked him to teach her about God and help her to grow. He agreed, and they started having a Bible study together.

After a few weeks of the Bible study, her stepfather started molesting her. This continued for the next couple of years, until she finally broke. She went to a counselor at her school, and the story became known. The stepfather denied it, and her mother sided with him. Kendra left after high school to come to college, where she had been in private counseling, trying to recover, trying to come to an understanding of what had happened. This young lady, sexually abused by a stepfather who was a pastor, could not believe that becoming a Christian changed people—not in the deepest sense.

At the heart of her struggle lay these questions: Is God real? Is the Christian life simply religious propaganda? Is everyone in the church hypocritical or just struggling hard to be "nice" people? She wondered about the difference between *religion* and a *relationship with God*—also about the difference between *performing to please people* and *real change produced by God.*

Is a relationship with God that brings real change possible? That's the question for many Christians. During that semester something began to happen to Kendra. She began to hear clearly, as though for the first time, the message of life that Jesus offers. She began to understand that Jesus came to earth to bring her healing from her abuse, to give her the ability to forgive others for hurting her, to offer her a spiritual power that would help her overcome her past and help her find wholeness and health in every aspect of her life. She discovered in the message and ministry of Jesus that she could be different, that she could change, that she could become like Him.

Hindrances for the First Disciples . . . and For Us

Kendra is not unlike many of us. When we consider the possibility of changing, of becoming like Jesus, our unrealistic expectations, our experiences, our lack of training—not to mention our current cultural climate—can all work against us. We lack an understanding of spiritual growth and how it comes about in real life.

I've spent the last twenty years in a study of discipleship as it occurred in the ancient world, and specifically, how it appeared in the ministry of Jesus and the life of the early church. Jesus' earliest followers often failed to grow as they should have grown. Their self-centeredness caused them at times to quarrel over worldly ambition instead of following in Jesus' path of discipleship (Mark 10:35-45). At times they allowed the difficult circumstances of life to stifle their faith in His protecting care (Matthew 14:22-33).

Like us, the first disciples faced hindrances to their spiritual growth in Christ. What were these hindrances? How did they overcome them?

The disciples did not understand clearly who Jesus was. As the disciples followed Jesus, they grew to understand who He was. But very often, their own misconceptions got in the way. Peter gave some of the clearest statements of Jesus' identity—but immediately after confessing Jesus as "the Christ, the Son of the living God," Peter tried to stop Him from going to the cross (Matthew 16:16, 22-23). The Jesus for whom Peter had given up much to follow was going to rule Israel and drive out Roman oppressors, not suffer and die. This Jesus was going to fulfill Peter's plans and ease his frustrations—wasn't He?

Like Peter, many of us refuse to seek Jesus for who He really is and for what *He* wants to accomplish in our lives. We create a Jesus of our own making, a Jesus who will do everything we want Him to do.

It would take the most radical miracle in all of history, the Resurrection, to demonstrate to the disciples that Jesus was more than they imagined. He was God—and suddenly they knew He could bring about the changed lives He had promised. Only as we grasp Jesus' identity as the divine Messiah, the resurrected Lord who now dwells in our hearts through faith (Ephesians 3:17) and is actually present with us, can we open ourselves to Him in the gritty events of life.

I saw this recently in an older man who had spent most of his life attending church, singing in the choir, and serving on various boards. He had always been a gruff, self-sufficient sort, but when he faced the prospect of a very delicate surgery, he found himself afraid of the possible outcome. His pastor spent several long afternoons at his side in the hospital, helping him to understand that Jesus was actually present there at his side, and that He would be there through the surgery and recovery with comforting presence and enabling power. Those were not new words, but they struck home in a new way. It was as though he saw Jesus in a completely new light, not just as an ancient figure of history. He was right there in the hospital room to walk with him through the crisis. By seeing Jesus more clearly, this man was changed and enabled to face his surgery with confidence and courage. In fact, that experience changed him for the rest of his life. Jesus became to him a real, living presence.

They did not believe who they were to be as Jesus' disciples. Although Jesus' first followers had made a commitment to be His disciples, they did not at first believe that they could be forever changed by God *from* *the inside.* Early in His ministry Jesus had clarified that His form of discipleship would include spiritual regeneration (John 3:3), not simply external religious formalism.

Again, we see in Peter a man who tried desperately to live up to his calling as Jesus' disciple. He is notorious for his early inconsistency and for the way he denied Jesus at the cross. But it is this same Peter who would later encourage exiled believers to be faithful during their persecution, declaring, "For you have been born again, not of perishable seed, but of imperishable, through the living and enduring word of God" (1 Peter 1:23). After surrendering his own plans and demands, he came to see that discipleship begins as an inner work in which God produces His eternal life in us. This is similar to John's realization that the true Christian is empowered to overcome sin and conquer the world because of the seed of God within us (compare 1 John 2:29; 3:9; 5:1-4, 18).[2]

The major focus of this book is to explore the ways that you and I can become like Jesus because God has planted in us the seeds of spiritual transformation. We can develop a pattern of life in which we intentionally allow God to transform us from the inside out. People who are changed in heart—this is what describes Jesus' followers, and it's what marks the radical nature of biblical Christianity.

The disciples did not know what was available to them to help them as children of God. The disciples had looked to Jesus for strength and leadership for several years. But when He was arrested and crucified, they had nowhere to turn. Jesus' earlier promise to send another Comforter must have seemed like wishful thinking. They hid when Jesus was led to the cross. Even after they heard of His resurrection they hid away in fear for their own lives (John 20:19). They did not yet fully know what was available to them to live courageously and victoriously in a hostile world.

With the coming of the Holy Spirit at Pentecost, the ancient promise of the prophet Joel and Jesus' own promise became a reality (Acts 2:16 and following verses; John 14:15-17). The Holy Spirit was the gift to everyone who called upon the name of Jesus for salvation (Acts 2:38-39), who now provided the boldness to preach and heal, the courage to stand up under persecution, and the power to experience transformation in their personal characteristics and values.

The apostle Paul understood the difference that the Holy Spirit could make in a person's life. He, himself, was transformed from one who breathed murderous threats against the disciples and who tried to wipe out the new movement (Acts 8:1; 9:1-2) to one who was willing to die for Jesus. Paul also prayed that his readers would know in their personal experience the power of the Spirit, the same power that raised Jesus from the dead (Ephesians 1:18-20).

Do you lack this power? Do your habits of life defeat your every attempt to experience new life? Do you wish that you could give your children a better example of a godly life? In later chapters we will give direct attention to understanding and practicing a life in the Spirit. We will see that life in the Spirit will bring realistic change in every area of our lives, helping us to become the kind of people Jesus desires us to be.

The disciples did not grasp their calling. The disciples had heard Jesus declare that the kingdom of God was at hand (Mark 1:15), but in their initial self-centeredness they often turned this around to mean privilege and position for themselves (Mark 10:35). They did not yet fully understand that God's children are not called simply for their own comfort and benefit. We are called to be ambassadors of the kingdom of God. We are to demonstrate the message of transformation to a world stuck in its compulsions, fear, anger, lust, and sin.

When the first disciples encountered their risen Master, they looked with a new light upon the part of His earthly mission that led Him to the cross. Jesus had not come to be served but to serve (Mark 10:45). His purpose was to go to the cross to bear the sins of the world and to show the disciples how to surrender their own lives so they could take up God's will for them—their own "cross." Knowing that God had a good and loving purpose, they could submit their wills and lives to the Father. In doing so, they would actually find real life (Matthew 16:24-27), and they began to work out their calling in the real world.

To go the way of the cross, to enter the process of surrendering everything to God—that is what forms our spirits in the image of Jesus in this thing called Christian discipleship. It will cost us everything. The cross always points to the empty tomb and resurrection life.

Owning Up to Our Responsibility

Kendra, like those first disciples, could not see Jesus clearly at first. Because of her stepfather's abuse and betrayal, she didn't trust anyone—why would she trust God and surrender her life to Him? Her painful experience caused her to think that the Christian life was a sham. The resulting bitterness and depression made her think she would never be emotionally or spiritually healthy.

During that semester I wanted her to see and hear Jesus. I wanted her to experience His love for her. I shared with her my own life, how I had been hurt, and angry, and bitter, and hateful. But when I came to really understand and experience Jesus' love, I became a different person. Many people had told me I would never be able to overcome the negative influences of my old life. But giving ourselves back to God, in the manner of Jesus, makes change possible. Real change can be found through living on this higher plane of existence. We can allow God to help us go beyond our natural impulses and past experiences, and instead live out His loving, giving, reconciling life through us.

Living with an awareness of God's presence, we are actually enabled by the Holy Spirit to live like Jesus. We can love others with His love, forgive in the way that He has forgiven us, and we can experience a transformation of our character. Then the fruit of the Spirit becomes a reality, not simply words on a written page.

I told Kendra that the ability to experience God's life in us is not something deeply mystical, intended only for a select few. Rather, it's what all Christians are called to experience.

Kendra took my challenge to open herself to God in a new way. Toward the end of that semester she sent me a letter, part of which I'll share.

> Dr. W.:
> I think I get it now—the Christian life. It's knowing God and actually having His life in me. Your challenge to me yesterday was really to live beyond the natural (hatred, bitterness, etc.) in relation to my folks. And I guess that's really what it's all about—living beyond what's natural. And I guess that explains why not every Christian seems like a Christian. That kind of life is so radical. Incredible! Anybody can hate their parents, or someone else, for hurting them so bad, but what if I stood up all alone and asked God to help me love them? . . . God in me—that's too incredible!

Kendra has since graduated, married, and finished graduate work in counseling. She has continued to work through her past and is now using it to help others who have had similar experiences. Through a Christian counselor she and her husband were brought together with her parents. After a heart-wrenching session, her stepfather confessed his earlier actions. This has opened up even more issues, including her mother's need to come to terms with her past actions. But a deep healing process has begun, all because the seed of new life that was planted in Kendra had begun to change her.

Ready to Begin

Maybe you have been a Christian for years. Or perhaps you are brand new to the faith. Do you want to experience change, growth, and inner strength? You can.

Becoming like Jesus *is* possible. For that reason God has placed a longing for transformation in our hearts. Consider the words Thomas Chisholm wrote for the hymn "O to be like Thee":

O to be like Thee! Blessed Redeemer,
This is my constant longing and prayer.
Gladly I'll forfeit all of earth's treasures,
Jesus, Thy perfect likeness to wear.

O to be like Thee! O to be like Thee,
Blessed Redeemer, pure as Thou art!
Come in Thy sweetness, come in Thy fullness;
Stamp Thine own image deep on my heart.

While we pursue this goal together, keep those words close to your heart as a confident prayer of assurance. Jesus takes us exactly as He finds us and transforms us into His likeness.

CHAPTER TWO

Am I a True Disciple?

For this cause let us be Jesus' disciples,
and let us learn to lead Christian lives.
For whoever is called by any name other
than this is not of God.

IGNATIUS OF ANTIOCH,
LETTER TO THE MAGNESIANS (CIRCA A.D. 110)[1]

■

The first time I put on a baseball uniform I was nine years old. Something happened to me the moment I put on that scratchy, ill-fitting shirt and pants. I was changed.

You see, I'd been chosen to play on the "Devil Dogs," a little league baseball team sponsored by a local Marine Corps unit. I was the youngest player on the team, not really up to the playing caliber of the bigger boys. I couldn't throw as hard, run as fast, or hit as well. But when I put on that uniform . . . I belonged!

In my heart—with *all* my heart—I wanted to be a "Dog." It meant that the big, athletic-looking men who coached the team approved and accepted me. It meant I was now in a place where someone would also coach me to throw, hit, steal bases, and spit like the bigger kids I admired. I was "in" and now I could grow and change in skill to become a real ball player. The uniform was outward evidence of the full intent and desire of my heart—to be, yes, a real "Dog."

To put on the uniform was to cross an invisible boundary line—to go from being a baseball player in my heart to entering into a process of becoming one out there on a real, dusty baseball field. Now I was "in the game." I would have to prove and improve my abilities to act out the intent of my heart for all to see.

In a similar way, making a commitment to follow Christ as His disciple begins with a true desire in our hearts. And then it must be proved and improved out on the playing field of the world. You cannot "act out" or fake the part of a disciple, just as you cannot fake being a ball player. The challenges of life will find you out for sure. This leads to my point.

Too often in the Christian church, we impose on people the "uniform," that is, outward behaviors that reflect what we think a Christian should look and act like. But the marks of a Christian disciple originate within, as attitudes of the heart. Too often, we insist on an external gauge of discipleship—how much someone witnesses, how many Scripture verses they can memorize—when we should be training people how to be changed in heart. A focus on externals encourages a shallow discipleship. Then we wonder why Christians wear out, get bored, or become discouraged when God is not working in their lives. You see, sometimes our focus on externals can even prevent real inner growth.

Boundary Markers in the Church

Displaying a fish with the letters ΙΧΘΥΣ on your car can be a positive way of demonstrating your commitment to Christ. But if we demanded that all Christians display a fish sign as a true mark of commitment to Christ, it would be absurdly legalistic! And it would easily lead to the creation of Christian "posers," that is, people who look and talk like devout Christians when they are with other Christians, but who act like any other person of the world when they are out of Christian company. They would put on external appearances in order to be accepted by the Christian group, adopting a set of highly visible, relatively superficial characteristics. Unfortunately, a number of superficial boundary markers have been established around what it means to be a disciple of Jesus.

What is your mental image of a disciple of Jesus? What do you think a true disciple should be? What should she act like? What should his lifestyle be like? At times we are more concerned that people conform to our image of a disciple than we are for them to be the kind of disciple that Jesus intended them to be.

In my early days as a Christian I belonged to different college campus ministries. Each group had its own special emphasis. One group emphasized that we should go out on a regular basis to witness to students on the campus. Another group emphasized that we should be actively involved in Scripture memorization and personal devotions. Another group regularly sponsored debates between Christians and nonChristians to help us sharpen our understanding of the Christian faith. Each group called its activities "discipleship" training and seemed to think that its way was the "right" way. I was helped tremendously by each group, but I also found myself confused as to what a true disciple of Jesus was to look and act like. There was a subtle suggestion that if I did not conform to the prescribed practices of a particular group, I wasn't a "real" disciple.

A flood of discipleship materials has swept over the church in the past forty years. And yet people today still seem very confused about what it means to be a disciple of Jesus Christ. In most of my speaking engagements in churches, retreats, and conferences in the last twenty years, I've asked the participants two questions.

> *How many of you can say, in the humble confidence of your heart, that you are convinced you are a true disciple of Jesus Christ? Please raise your hand.*

People are visibly confused as they attempt to answer the question. Most don't put their hand up at all, some do so hesitantly.

Then I ask:

> *How many of you can say, in the humble confidence of your heart, that you are convinced you are a true Christian? Please raise your hand.*

Immediately, most hands shoot up. No hesitation, no doubt! They are sure about being a Christian, but they are confused as to whether or not they are a disciple of Jesus.

I suggest that our image of a Christian disciple is often clouded by the variety of external markers offered as the sign of a true follower of Jesus. Which of the following has influenced your image of discipleship?[2]

The learner. Some emphasize that a disciple is the person who is dedicated to an intense study of the Bible. A disciple is actively involved in personal devotional time, Bible memorization, and Bible study as a regular habit of life. This implies that a Christian becomes a disciple when she is dedicated to learning the Word of God and applying it.

The committed. Others emphasize that a disciple is supremely committed to Christ. He has rejected a worldly lifestyle and is one of the truly dedicated ones at church or in the parachurch group. This means that a Christian is a disciple if he has truly denied himself material gains, worldly pursuits (like a career and/or hobbies) and spends all his time in and around church.

The worker. Still others declare that a disciple is actively involved in Christian service. Their service distinguishes them from nominal Christians who attend the group or church. This implies that a Christian becomes a disciple when he is an active worker for Christ.

The mentor. Some of us have been involved in one-on-one relationships in which an older, more mature Christian has "discipled" us. This is often called "mentoring." Many people believe that when we are involved in such a coaching, guiding relationship we have experienced true discipleship.

The small-group member. Small groups are one of the most effective means of facilitating growth in Christians because we can learn from the example of others, we can open our lives up to others, and we can be held accountable to the growth that we say we desire. Some suggest that even as Jesus discipled His small band of followers, true discipleship occurs today only when we are involved in a small group.

A Christian Is a Disciple of Jesus Christ

There is, of course, some truth in each of these and other models of discipleship. True, each can contribute to growth as a disciple, but none of them is the way that we *become a disciple*. That is, you can become a good learner, sacrificer, worker-servant, mentor, or group-attender and not necessarily develop the *heart* of a Christian disciple. I believe this is a major root of confusion today about discipleship. And it helps to explain why many people are frustrated in their Christian life.

The way a person *becomes* a disciple of Jesus is by confessing to Him and committing to Him as Savior and God. In fact, when you became a Christian, you answered the first call of the disciple, the invitation to put aside your own attempts to save yourself and to lead your life your own way.

Now the way you *grow* as a disciple is another matter. Study, spiritual fellowship, service, and many other things will come into play in support of your choice. But we must be clear that they are not the ways that you *become* a disciple. You become a Christian disciple by choosing to follow Christ in such a way that your core ambitions are changed, so you are no longer serving self first but God. Then your process of growth as a Christian is called discipleship.

Right now, you may or may not be actively growing as Jesus' disciple. But if you have entered into a salvation relationship with Jesus, He counts you as His disciple. And He has made a way for you to grow and to change to become like Him.

Discipleship for All Christians

It comes down to this: If we do not consider ourselves disciples, then we do not recognize that the discipleship teaching Jesus gave in His earthly ministry is directed to us. We think that it is directed only toward those specially committed persons. Discipleship becomes optional instead of a natural and normal part of the Christian life.

Kendra, who had been molested by her pastor stepfather, was convinced that being a Christian did not make a real difference in a person's life. Her experiences at home and church convinced her that the Christian faith produced no change, no significant difference between the daily life of a Christian and the daily life of a nonChristian. But she came to understand that she is Jesus' disciple. And the ways Jesus helped the earliest disciples to grow and change are also the ways in which He will help her to grow and change. Then she was able to enter into a dynamic relationship with Jesus, knowing that He offers a realistic means of transformation, from the inside out.

When Jesus issued the Great Commission (Matthew 28:19-20), He gave us two simple qualifications for discipleship. First, a disciple is born by the new birth of salvation when he or she responds to the gospel message. This marks disciples off from the world—especially as they declare their new life in Christ by being baptized in the name of the Father, Son, and Holy Spirit. Second, disciples grow as they are taught to obey all that Jesus commanded in His earthly ministry. Jesus' teaching touches on every area of life. And as we understand His teachings, allowing them to change our core motivations, we grow as disciples.

In later chapters we will examine closely what it means to grow as a disciple. But it is also important to understand the end goal of our growth. It is not merely that we should be "better" or "nicer" or "more zealous" people. No, Jesus gave us the true goal when He said that "[a disciple] who is fully trained will be like his [master]" (Luke 6:40, emphasis added).

Discipleship *is* the Christian life. And the goal of the Christian life is to become like Jesus.

So now I ask the question of you: "Can you say, in the humble confidence of your heart, that you are a true disciple of Jesus Christ? And are you willing to grow and become more like Him day by day?"

If you are a Christian, you should be waving your hand! And now we can embark together on the path of discipleship—becoming like Jesus!

CHAPTER THREE

Take a Good Look at Jesus

Future historians are likely to conclude that the more we knew about Jesus the less we knew Him, and the more precisely His words were translated the less we understood or heeded them.

MALCOLM MUGGERIDGE,
JESUS: THE MAN WHO LIVES[1]

■

"For to me, to live is Christ, and to die is gain" (Philippians 1:21).

This remarkable statement was penned by the apostle Paul while he was imprisoned. "To die is gain" is more easily understood when we realize how strongly Paul trusted in the promise of glory that awaited him after death.

But what did Paul mean when he said, "For to me, to live is Christ"? Perhaps you've heard those words before. Perhaps they are even so familiar that they don't really penetrate to your own world.

What would it mean for you and me to say, "For me to live is Christ"? How would you apply those words on a moment-by-moment basis? Could we possibly say that those words characterize our life at home, at school, at work, on the playing field, on the freeway?

For Paul, Christ had become both the pathway and the goal of his life and ministry. To become like Christ was the motive of his actions, the source of his strength and joy, the center of his life. Christ's values had become Paul's. Christ's character was now Paul's highest aspiration. Christ's very life was now Paul's.

Paul made a parallel statement earlier in his ministry:

> I have been crucified with Christ; and it is no longer I who live, but Christ lives in me; and the life which I now live in the flesh I live by faith in the Son of God, who loved me and delivered Himself up for me. (Galatians 2:20, NASB)

This does not negate Paul's individuality and identity. Rather, he was enabled, through the presence of Christ in his life, to be all that God had intended for him. Paul was now able to fulfill his life's highest potential and transformation *because* for him to live was Christ.

In chapter one, we saw that the earliest disciples began to experience personal transformation when they clearly understood Jesus' identity. Today we cannot live as Christ, we cannot become like Him, until Christ's life becomes our very own. But who is Jesus, really? What does He have to offer that really could make a difference in my modern life and yours?

When we try to grasp who Jesus is, we run into some immediate difficulties. For many of us our understanding of Jesus is cluttered with fragmented or wrong images of Him. We are often more familiar with the pieces of Jesus' image that our culture, denomination, church, or fellowship group excised for its own uses than we are with the full biblical picture of Jesus. What follows are a few of the fragmentary images of Jesus that can keep us from seeing the whole, true person of Christ.

Sunday School Images of Jesus

My wife, Lynne, was raised in a strong Christian home and grew up in a solid Bible-teaching church. Even so, she had a Sunday school picture of Jesus that was not adequate for helping her to "live Christ." We saw that several years ago when we were going through a particularly difficult time. Our children were in the junior high and high school years. We were struggling financially and so I was working longer hours on a regular basis than I should. Then a "friend" said some really hateful things to Lynne. Not unusual problems, but altogether they made for a difficult time.

When I tried to encourage Lynne, I reminded her that in all of our difficulties she needed to remember that Jesus understands. He lived a human life, and He can give us strength in the middle of everything we go through.

"Well, I'm not sure I exactly understand all of that," she responded.

"Jesus was *God.* He wasn't married, and He never had any children. He died when He was around thirty. He didn't have to be forty years old, or a woman who is trying to pull all of life together!"

Now, you have to understand, Lynne is a godly woman, but she doesn't like cliché answers or "God talk." She saw my advice more as a religious pacifier than a concrete solution to the struggles of everyday life.

Lynne's response is not unlike many others. From the time she was a young child, her mind picked up an understanding of Jesus that was so exalted, holy, and sublime that He could not be human enough to relate to her world.

Another "Sunday school image" of Jesus goes in the other direction. Philip Yancey writes, "I first got acquainted with Jesus when I was a child, singing 'Jesus Loves Me' in Sunday school, addressing bedtime prayers to 'Dear Lord Jesus,' watching Bible Club teachers move cutout figures across a flannelgraph board. I associated Jesus with Kool-Aid and sugar cookies and gold stars for good attendance."[2] Here is an image of Jesus so meek and mild that He cannot powerfully challenge us in our lives, let alone stand up to the powers of this world.

Jesus is fully God; and when He came to earth He also became fully human. Understanding the union of those two natures in one person is one of our most challenging pursuits. The more we open ourselves to understanding that the God who became man wants to live in us, the richer will be our experience of the Christian life.

Sectarian Varieties of Jesus

The images of Jesus we carry around are also as numerous as the groups from which we come. Individual churches and denominations and parachurch organizations tend to focus on certain characteristics of Jesus. Usually, they choose those characteristics that support their own understanding of their mission. These stereotypes give some slice of the truth about Jesus but often do not tell the whole story. And so they hinder full growth because they do not open up to their members a complete picture of Jesus.

What comes into your mind first when you hear the name *Jesus*?

- Do you think of Jesus primarily as your *Savior*, the One who died on the cross to pay for your sins?

- Is Jesus first in your mind a *shepherd*, gathering little ones around Him as the gentle shepherd gathers little lambs?
- Perhaps you picture Jesus primarily as the *teacher* who called disciples and trained them to make other disciples.
- Or is Jesus *Lord*—the God of the universe who has all power and authority over nature, nations, and peoples?
- Does the thought of Jesus as *friend* come first to mind, the One who understands and comforts you?
- Or do you first of all picture Jesus as a *revolutionary*, One who pronounced woes on the Pharisees and cleansed the temple?
- Is Jesus the great *provider* who came to meet needs?

A balanced, rounded understanding of Jesus needs to incorporate all aspects of His character and nature. Basing our Christian life on a partial image of Him can never provide a complete picture of what we can become because it offers only a limited understanding of what Jesus can supply to us.

For instance, if Jesus is only *friend* to you, perhaps you do not understand that He is also the powerful Lord of the universe who can supply you with the power necessary to accomplish whatever God calls you to in life. If Jesus is only your *gentle shepherd*, perhaps you do not recognize Him as the spiritual revolutionary who despised religious hypocrisy.

We need a full awareness of Jesus in order to accept *all* of the roles that He desires to play in our lives.

Cultural Counterfeits of Jesus

According to a recent nationwide survey conducted by the Barna Research Group, two of every five people surveyed believe Jesus sinned while on earth. Twenty-seven percent of Christians and 30 percent of church attendees believe He committed sin.[3]

I was stunned to see this statistic. The Bible clearly teaches that Jesus did *not* sin (Hebrews 4:15). Why do so many people believe He did? Primarily because they are influenced significantly by a major shift in the cultural perception of Jesus, especially in the popular media. Various influences—such as liberal theology, other world religions, and materialistic science—have moved our culture away from Judeo-Christian values. The further we get from biblical moorings, the more confused and relativistic people are about Jesus. We must be alert to the fact that different world views are vying to dominate our culture. These views have affected the way people perceive Jesus and have even permeated the church.[4] The Bible clearly teaches that Jesus came to conquer sin and death. And in so doing, Jesus now offers us the means to be free from sin's power over us (Romans 6). Your perception of Jesus matters a great deal, both theologically and practically.

A Picture of the Real Jesus

If we are to become like Jesus we must be clear about who He is and not be limited by our own views or fooled by cultural counterfeits. If we go too far in one direction, we minimize His deity so that He is not powerful enough to conquer sin or enable us to live transformed lives. If we go too far in the other direction, we minimize His humanness so that He cannot really be an example of how to live a truly human life. A good look at Jesus in fullness and truth is what we need. As he begins his classic work, *The Imitation of Christ*, Thomas à Kempis writes:

> 'He that followeth Me, walketh not in darkness,' saith the Lord. These are the words of Christ, by which we are taught, how we ought to imitate His life and manners, if we will be truly enlightened, and be delivered from all blindness of heart. Let therefore our chief endeavor be, to meditate upon the life of Jesus Christ.[5]

Let's look closely at some specific ways in which Jesus' life challenges and encourages us as growing human beings and children of God.

Jesus Was a Whole Person

Scripture tells us that Jesus "grew in wisdom and stature, and in favor with God and men" (Luke 2:52). Jesus was not some isolated mystic; rather, He developed all aspects of human life. And so, I believe, He *honored* all aspects of our humanity.

Jesus grew in . . .

- Wisdom = Intellectually
- Stature = Physically
- Favor with God = Spiritually
- Favor with men = Socially/Emotionally

Ultimately, healthy discipleship means full human development, as God intended in our original creation. (In chapter eight we will consider more fully the implications of this development, how the entire person is brought into conformity to the image of Christ.) A severely limited view of discipleship restricts our growth to only one or two areas of human life. For instance, some view discipleship simply as study and a mental exercise. Others view discipleship as a "spiritual" exercise, somehow separate from the social dimensions of life. But in Jesus, we see the development of every area of life.

Jesus' Spirit-Empowered Life

Jesus was fully God with all of the attributes of deity, but He limited their use so that he could live the same kind of life that you and I live.[6] In a general way, the power for Jesus' earthly life came from the Holy Spirit (Acts 2:22; 10:38). He limited His powers to those of a human and then drew upon the Holy Spirit for strength for His life. In this way He could give us the perfect example of the Spirit-led life. The beginning of Jesus' public ministry was marked by the Spirit coming upon Him at baptism (Mark 1:9-11) and then leading Him to the desert where He was tempted (Mark 1:12-13). And it was the Spirit to whom Jesus turned in His humanity to receive power to withstand Satan's temptations.

What this shows us is that we, as humans, can live the way God intended us to live. The Spirit that enabled Jesus to overcome the world is available to us today. Few of us may perform extraordinary miracles—unless that is God's will for our lives—but we can all live in minute-by-minute dependence on the Spirit in every area of life.

How Jesus lived in the Spirit can be seen as we look more closely at His life.

Jesus' Lifestyle

When we search the biblical record we see that Jesus not only lived in communion with the Father but in communion with the deepest needs of people in the gritty circumstances of life. Christians throughout the centuries have used Jesus' example as a model for developing in the spiritual life.[7] Here are some of the most important aspects of His life:

1. Jesus lived in intimate relationship with His Father. This intimacy is modeled for us in His practice of prayer and in His

teaching on prayer (Luke 5:16). This intimacy with God is available to us today, even as the Spirit helps us in our prayer life. Paul tells us that we don't often know how to pray, so we rely on the Spirit to intercede for us (Romans 8:26-27).

2. Jesus was empowered by the Holy Spirit, and He promised us the comfort and the power of the Spirit after His departure (Mark 1:8, 9, 12; John 14:12-17). One of the unmistakable marks of the earliest church was this empowering by the Spirit (Acts 1:8). The Spirit's power is promised to each believer today (Ephesians 4:29-32, 5:18-21). The very reason why you and I are able to say "no" to temptations is because the Spirit helps us to take God's way (see 1 Corinthians 10:13).
3. At the very beginning of Jesus' ministry, we see Him involved in spiritual warfare, as Satan tempts Him to depart from the Father's will for His earthly ministry (Matthew 4:1-11). Spiritual warfare is a daily reality for each of us (Ephesians 6:10-12,13). Jesus shows the importance of a life governed by the Word of God in order to become pure in heart (Matthew 5:1-12).
4. Jesus expressed the full range of human emotions—from joy (Hebrews 12:2) to anger[8] (John 11:33, Mark 11:15-17), from compassion (Matthew 9:35-38; Luke 19:41) to frustration (Matthew 17:17). He experienced sorrow (John 11:35) and love (John 11:5,13:34-35). He becomes for us the example of how to express our human emotions in a healthy manner. This includes times when we can express ourselves with our tears and times when we express ourselves through our laughter. It includes caring for our closest friends, as well as caring for the sick, needy, and neighbors.[9]
5. Jesus came to earth to bring the message of salvation. He came to seek the lost and sinners (Mark 2:13-17). His teaching was based on Scripture, but He brought an authority which astounded the crowds (Matthew 7:28; Mark 1:21-28). Like the early church, we have in Jesus a clear example of both actions and words we can use as we reach out to a lost world (Acts 1:8, Colossians 3:16).
6. Jesus lived in a way that did not focus on His own comforts. He came to serve, not to be served (Mark 10:45). During His

final night on earth He washed the disciples' feet and said: "I have set you an example that you should do as I have done for you" (John 13:15). If our Teacher and Lord could serve His disciples, then as His disciples we must serve each other. Jesus did not amass material riches or possessions, and He taught the dangers of wealth (Matthew 6:19-24). This does not require us to become paupers or live in caves, but it does tell us we are not to live only to advance our own comforts. Even the work of our hands has a goal, and that is to have resources we can share with those in need (Ephesians 4:28).

7. Jesus was involved with a community of faith as a normal part of His life. His disciples were His family of faith (Matthew 12:46-50). Jesus extended the view of family to include our relationships with others who believe in and serve Him. The family of God is reflected in the local church, the community of faith in the world today (1 Timothy 3:4-5, James 2:15-17). Loneliness is a difficult experience of life for many people. But the family of faith can provide companions for older believers, an understanding ear for a disturbed high schooler, and support and direction for parents trying to raise children in this challenging world.
8. Jesus concentrated many of His efforts on preparing a new generation who could continue His work once He had passed from the earthly phase of His ministry (Mark 3:13-19). Whether laity or clergy, we are called to birth and train the next generation of Christians (2 Timothy 2:1-2).

Jesus' Virtues

We could enumerate the virtues of Jesus' life simply by quoting the fruit of the Spirit as delineated by the apostle Paul: love, joy, peace, patience, kindness, goodness, faithfulness, gentleness and self-control (Galatians 5:22-23). The virtues of Jesus' life have been described by Michael Griffiths as the *Colours of His Life*.[10] Like a rainbow, these interior attributes add beauty, power, and depth to the stories of the New Testament.

The next time you read the Gospels, be alert for these qualities in Jesus: service (Mark 10:45), patience and endurance (Hebrews 12:1-2), suffering (Luke 9:22-23, 1 Thessalonians 1:6), gentleness (Matthew

11:29; 21:5), humility (Matthew 11:29, Philippians 2:8), obedience (Luke 2:51, John 4:34), and love (John 13:34-35, 11:5).

The spiritual qualities of Jesus' life are character traits that the Holy Spirit can form in us. Later, we will look closely at these traits—Jesus' spiritual makeup—because it is these qualities that God wants to recreate in us as disciples.

The Balanced Spiritual Life

As we take a good look at Jesus we find that He invites us to follow Him into the most abundant life available to humanity (John 10:7-10). That is because He leads us into a satisfying, balanced life that is also lived in service to God.

Each of us tends to be more naturally inclined toward one aspect of Jesus' life or another. Some of us are naturally inclined toward building community and relationships with believers. Others are more naturally expressive of our emotions and drawn toward support groups or worship teams, while others are more servant-like in our natural makeup. We can build upon our strengths, and then concentrate on areas where we need to grow. This allows Jesus to lead us into a more balanced Christian life.

The more we know Jesus, understanding how He balances and fills our lives, the more you and I become like Him.

In any relationship, knowing another person must be counterbalanced with *being known.* If we are to know Jesus more intimately, we will learn to open ourselves to being known by Him, and that will mean allowing Him to examine our motives, goals, and priorities. This begins the road to true inner freedom, which is one of our greatest blessings in Christ. He will open us up so that the deepest places within us are made clean and healthy—and so that we are more and more like Jesus Himself.

It is as we walk this road—knowing and being known—that we will be able to say with the apostle Paul, "For to me, to live is Christ."

CHAPTER FOUR

THE REAL IMITATION: THE "NONNEGOTIABLES" OF BIBLICAL DISCIPLESHIP

When the Bible speaks of following Jesus, it is proclaiming a discipleship which will liberate mankind from all man-made dogmas, from every burden and oppression, from every anxiety and torture which afflicts the conscience.

DIETRICH BONHOEFFER,
THE COST OF DISCIPLESHIP (A.D. 1937)[1]

■

A young man who is a relatively new Christian recently asked me, "What does the Bible mean when it talks about us being 'conformed' to Christ? That sounds like making us all into robots!" Like most of us, he doesn't like the thought of losing his individuality—that is, his personality, ambitions, and the like—and mechanistically, passionlessly to take on someone else's agenda for his life. Sadly, too often in Christianity we have taken a cookie-cutter approach to Christian discipleship. We have tried to force-fit individuals, men, women, and young people, into a simplistic, one-size-fits-all image of what a true disciple of Jesus says and does.

What God does with us is wonderfully different. As we learn to relax and trust Him with the full childlike trust of Jesus, He wants to bring us to the fullest expression of our uniqueness. We don't become Jesus, we become *like* Jesus, the perfect example of what God intended for humanity under the influence of God. Only in this arrangement, in fact, can our individuality be retained and given its truest expression.

So, when Paul said "be imitators of me, just as I also am of Christ" (1 Corinthians 11:1, NASB), he was not suggesting that we become clones of himself or Jesus, void of personhood. Rather the "real imitation" is a person who takes the example of Jesus seriously, and who is transformed from the inside out by the Spirit of God. This person is the one who can become more true to his or her potential as a real person than ever before.

But for this kind of discipleship to occur we need examples, both the example of Jesus, and the example of other "Pauls" around us. Discipleship is a process by which we *imitate-as-we-are-transformed*; the process by which we *imitate-in-order-to-be-transformed.*

In this chapter we will take an overview of the popular understanding of what it is to be a disciple of Jesus. We'll also look at the general principles we need to act upon if we are to grow as disciples. In order to do so, we may need to face some general misconceptions that keep us from accepting a fuller, richer understanding of the believer's growth in Christ. So, before we move on, think through the following questions:

- What is your understanding of discipleship? What does discipleship "look" like? Where does it occur? What is its goal?
- If you were going to be discipled by someone, who would you choose? Why?
- If you wanted to disciple someone else, who would you want to disciple? What would you do?
- If you were to develop a discipleship program in your church, or on your campus, or in your neighborhood, what would it look like? What would its goals be?

The Challenge—Really Lost Humans

The truth is, each of us has an image of what a disciple is to be like, how he or she should act, what lifestyle he or she should live. That is, most of us have an end goal in mind, for example, an evangelist, a youth worker, a pastor, the head of women's ministries, or a minister to the needs of the poor. None of those goals is bad, but what do we do if a person shows no interest in heading toward our vision of a true disciple? Do we shrug him off, dismiss him as not worth our time and efforts? It's true, there is a time and place and need for training Christian workers. But it's also true that the calling of Christian disciples can begin out among people who, initially, show no interest in the gospel-spreading tasks that have become second nature in our evangelical culture.

In our family, we have witnessed the important work of God that needs to be done in this world among young people who are suffering the effects of a culture that is in spiritual and moral disintegration. The fundamental support system of these young people, their own family, is in such a state of collapse that they have little or no real life guidance. Seeing ourselves surrounded by a number of such young people in our California beach town, Lynne and I realized that a stage was set for us on which we could live out the challenge of discipling kids whose understanding of home, family, love, trust, and commitment had been shaken or destroyed.

Our call to discipleship among these young people came naturally enough. At first, in fact, we found ways to get involved with our daughters' friends because we wanted to stay close to our own teenagers. To be honest, it was also a lot of fun.

One summer, for instance, I'd get up at 6:30 every Tuesday. Our older daughter, Michelle, and I would pick up between six and sixteen of her friends to go surfing. Afterwards, we'd go out for breakfast. Such strong bonds were built with these kids that hardly a day went by when I came home from the seminary that I didn't find wet suits and boards on the porch, and kids inside having a snack. Lynne became "Mom" to many of these kids, as she listened to them pour out confusion and heartaches, as she offered support and guidance. We were even there to cheer them on at surfing competitions.

Likewise, when our younger daughter, Wendy, became involved in competitive volleyball, Lynne and I sometimes found ourselves in the role of surrogate parents. Whether we were traveling to a national competition or munching on bowls of popcorn on our sofa, we counseled on everything from dating to parents, nutrition to college and life goals.

Today, many of these kids are adults, and some are married with children of their own. A few are Christians, actively pursuing growth in Christ. Others are not but show the signs of waking up to their spiritual needs. We certainly hope that more and more of them will make the commitment to follow Christ. But even that is not exactly why I have told these brief stories.

It was mostly in hindsight that Lynne and I realized our discipling role in its broadest sense, that we were pouring unconditional love into the lives of these young people whom God loves. Most of them were from broken or unstable homes, with parents who were preoccupied with sifting through the troubles of their own lives. They had never seen a home where the foundation of commitment to Christ led to a loving commitment in marriage and a commitment to raise stable and well-loved children. They had never experienced patient listening and careful guidance. They had never encountered healthy, loving confrontation for poor decisions. The bottom line was that they had never experienced unqualified support as human beings with complicated needs. Not only that, but very few of these kids came from families that went to church—or even believed in God. It was always clear that our family was under careful scrutiny. They wanted to see if we were Christians in name only, or if we were genuine lovers of God and people.

In the end, we realized that the kind of discipling we had done was probably very different from the kind of discipleship program we often think of. The setting wasn't a church but our everyday lives. The teaching tools were our attitudes and commitments, our words and actions toward each other. The ones being discipled were not those who signed up for the class, but "whosoever" would come and be part of our family. Our excitement is based on this: As these young people face careers, marriage, and parenting, they will reach down inside themselves for some healthy standard of how to *do* life. And as real life presses in, they will remember a time and place where they saw God's love lived out in a family and given to them unconditionally. So the story is far from over because for some, it has yet to be written.

The Enticement of Programs

Perhaps it's obvious that I believe discipleship needs to take place in the context of everyday life. As a New Testament scholar, I believe this to be true with every fiber of my being.

This points to one of the real dangers of any kind of discipleship program: If we focus so much on form and practice, we often lose sight of the goal. Programs can help by giving us tangible methods and outcomes. Programs can be effective in transferring knowledge, training certain behaviors, or producing other program leaders. But programs can also entice us to elevate methods and forms above the goal of transformed people. Programs can focus more on external behavior as a means of evaluating growth. This cookie-cutter approach to discipleship expects everyone to look exactly like the model laid out by any particular program. We expect people to perform according to the outcome that our program lays out.

The apostle Paul pointed to Jesus as the ultimate example; for in all His attitudes, actions, words, and goals, He showed us humanity perfected by the indwelling of the Spirit of God. And then, in the confident sincerity of his heart, Paul said that he was living close to Jesus' example. He wasn't perfect, but he was the example of Jesus that the church needed to follow as they made the transition from their old pagan ways of life to new patterns of life as Christians. Paul encouraged these believers to be serious about their everyday choices before the Lord, to accept the differences they found among themselves and then to collectively seek to glorify God. He offered himself as an example of a mature believer who had wrestled with these life issues.

We all need examples. And if a program is really geared to helping us become stronger in the character of Jesus, then use it. But don't be enticed to insist on using a program which destroys the uniqueness of people or is a substitute for the living example of Jesus.

The Tendency Toward Institutionalism

There is another very real hazard for anyone involved in a discipleship relationship; that is, the danger of institutionalism.

Institutions are meant to promote the growth of individuals, to minister to individuals so that they are better equipped to handle life on their own. Institutions are a means to the end: The goal is a person who is equipped to walk with God through real life.

It is a tragedy, then, when our institutions become more important than the individual—when the individual is made to serve the institution. Then supporting the institution becomes the end, and the individual is the means to the end.

For example, I am ashamed to admit that when I was a pastor I was often more concerned with the attendance at church functions than I was with the personal growth of the people who attended. I evaluated my own success by how fast and how large the church grew. And because of that I wanted my people to give priority to church functions over anything else. Because my end goal was numbers, not always depth, I considered our church activities more important than the spiritual growth of the people who made up the church.

Think of the institutions or groups in which you are involved. Ask yourself these questions:

- Are we making people into disciples *of our institutions*, or are our institutions making people into *disciples of Jesus*?

- Are our disciples proficient at running *programs*, or at living a real *relationship* with Jesus?
- Does our attachment to our institutions *isolate* us from the world, or equip us for *changing* the world?
- Are people focusing on *us* because of the importance of our programs, or are we (and our programs) the "means to the end," so people see *Jesus* more clearly?

It is critical for us to examine our practices to see how institutional we are becoming. How does your church or your ministry, or even your own personal life, match up when examined against those questions?

Jesus established the church as His functioning body on the earth in His absence. As such, the church is an institution designed to draw people into a loving fellowship with Christ and His people, and to equip Christians to carry out the work of ministry (Ephesians 4:11-12). But it is possible for even our gospel-preaching churches and organizations to fall into the trap of cold, religious institutionalism, where the institution is the *end* instead of the *means* by which Christ is reproduced in us.

Our Call

In previous chapters we saw that discipleship is the domain of all true believers, not only those who are called to ministry or those who are exceptionally committed. A disciple is a convert to Christianity (Acts 6:1-7), a direct fulfillment of Jesus' intent in the Great Commission (Matthew 28:19-20). Hence, the discipleship teachings and challenges of Jesus are not intended for a few highly committed individuals. They are guidelines for living for all believers. We are not called to direct our families, friends, and coworkers into discipling programs, or to hand them over to institutions with good training materials. We are called to live as children of God, as imitators of Christ, so people around us can see the light in us and honor our Father in heaven (see Matthew 5:13-16).

This places a radical challenge before each believer. We are called to authentic Christian living, and in a way that sifts out those who have adopted a form of easy-believism.

Consider these definitions:

Disciple. A disciple is a *committed follower* of a great master. When Jesus arrived on the scene in the first century, there were many masters with their disciples. John the Baptist had his disciples (John 1:35; 3:25), the Pharisees had their disciples (Matthew 22:15-16), and various other kinds of religious and political masters had their disciples. A disciple was a person who had committed himself or herself to a master and the master's teachings, way of life, objectives, attitudes. The form of discipleship varied significantly according to the goals of the master.

Disciple of Jesus. In the specific sense of a disciple of Jesus we have a much more focused definition. Throughout His ministry Jesus clarified the goals and characteristics of His form of discipleship, so we can say that a disciple of Jesus *is a person who has been called by Jesus to eternal life, has claimed Him as Savior and God, and has embarked upon the life of following Him.* This is a relationship that has profound implications for everyday life.

Discipleship and discipling. Discipleship is the ongoing process of growth as a believer learns how to become like Jesus *in every area of life.* Discipling implies a responsibility to help one another grow in the imitation of Jesus. As we become more fully the human vessels God wants us to be, we are challenged by Jesus to continue our spiritual growth by investing in the lives of others.

Think through the following guideline for understanding the implications of these definitions for everyday life and ministry:

> Discipleship means living a fully human life in this world in union with Jesus Christ and His people, growing in conformity to His image, and helping others to know and become like Jesus.

Eyes on the Prize

The *goal* of biblical discipleship must not be confused with the *means of growth* into that goal. Our goal is to become like Jesus as the following passages indicate. I have added the emphasis to highlight the point:

- "A disciple, when fully *trained*, will be *like* the master." (see Luke 6:40, Matthew 10:24-25)
- ". . . until Christ is *formed* in you." (Galatians 4:19, NASB)
- "But we all, with unveiled face beholding as in a mirror the glory of the Lord, are being *transformed* into the same image from glory to glory, just as from the Lord, the Spirit." (2 Corinthians 3:18, NASB)

- "For those God foreknew he also predestined to be *conformed* to the likeness of his Son." (Romans 8:29)

We rest in the wonderful truth that becoming like Jesus is initiated and accomplished by God's work in our lives. Saint Cyril of Alexandria in the fifth century, commenting on how Jesus is formed in us, says:

> He is formed in us by the Spirit, who regenerates us to God through Himself. Since, therefore, we are formed to Christ, and He is signified in us and His image beautifully worked in us by the Spirit in a likeness according to nature, surely the Spirit is God.[2]

The various means by which the Spirit of God accomplishes this work can be summarized in the following passages:

- Disciples make new disciples: "Go therefore and make disciples of all the nations, . . . baptizing them in the name of the Father and the Son and the Holy Spirit, . . . teaching them to observe all things that I commanded you." (Matthew 28:19-20)
- The disciple is a new person, leaving behind his old life by putting on a new life. (Ephesians 4:20-24)
- Disciples are genuine if they are growing in the imitation of Jesus, our one true Master. (1 Corinthians 11:1)
- Disciples are in spiritual warfare. (Ephesians 6:10-12)
- Disciples prepare a new generation of leaders, men and women willing to give their all for the sake of God's kingdom. (2 Timothy 2:2)

As God Prompts Change, Obey Him

As Scripture teaches and Saint Cyril's comment implies, the life of a disciple of Jesus Christ is one in which we learn to balance the work of the Spirit of God with our own obedience.

To understand how this operates I offer three suggestions.

Keep an "Inside-Out" Mentality. Holding an "inside-out" mentality means that we begin by focusing on the inner person. That means growing in spiritual intimacy with Jesus. As we develop His trusting, obedient nature, inward changes in our attitude toward God and others will result in changes in our outer behavior, changes that can be seen in the actions of our body (Romans 6:12-14) or "flesh" (Galatians 5:16).

This stands in contrast to religious behavior. The Pharisees, for instance, were supremely dedicated and recognized as the most righteous people in Israel. That is why Jesus' statement in His Sermon on the Mount is so startling: "Unless your righteousness surpasses that of the Pharisees and the teachers of the law, you will certainly not enter the kingdom of heaven" (Matthew 5:20). Imagine the thoughts of the common people when they heard this. *How could I possibly surpass the righteousness of the Pharisees? I suppose this means I'll never be able to enter God's kingdom.* But the amazing truth of the gospel—the gospel of the kingdom—is that any person who comes to Jesus in faith receives a new life which begins in the heart and moves to transform the whole person. When the heart is surrendered to God, then the righteousness of any common disciple of Jesus surpasses that of the Pharisees because true righteousness begins on the inside. The Pharisees had a tendency to work from the outside in, expecting outward observance to produce inward change. That was why Jesus' most scathing criticisms were launched at the Pharisees, whose practice was to make the outside clean and beautiful, while their inner life—their connection to God—was dead.

> "Woe to you, teachers of the law and Pharisees, you hypocrites! You are like whitewashed tombs, which look beautiful on the outside but on the inside are full of dead men's bones and everything unclean. In the same way, on the outside you appear to people as righteous but on the inside you are full of hypocrisy and wickedness." (Matthew 23:27-28)

Jesus declared that the righteousness of the kingdom of heaven—that is, right living, right relationships, right actions—grow from the inside out. Personal transformation begins in the inner person through our understanding and response to the work of the Spirit of God, which then moves to produce change on the outside. We must develop an inside out mentality so that Spirit-produced growth of the inner person produces outward change and obedience.

When I was young I got into a bad habit of shoplifting. I wasn't hungry or desperately needy. I stole simply because I wanted what I saw. It didn't matter to me that it belonged to someone else. I only thought of myself. One day when I was thirteen I was caught shoplifting a bag of candy, and I was handed over to the police. Sitting in that patrol car I vowed to the policeman that I wouldn't shoplift again. And I didn't, because I was afraid of the consequences. However, in my heart I still wanted to steal from other people if I could get away with it. Instead of shoplifting, I changed the direction of my stealing. As I got older I freely lied on my expense reports, and I took company equipment for my own personal use. I had changed on the outside, but for a time, I was still a thief on the inside.

The real internal change came when I became a Christian. As I began to understand God's values from the Bible, I began to respect other people and their property. I also realized that God would provide for me and that the things I wanted could never satisfy. And more than that, I wanted to help other people instead of stealing from them for my own selfish desires. As my heart changed I wanted to change my actions. I no longer wanted to steal from anyone. In this way, my external behavior came in line with my inner convictions. Real change on the outside must begin with a change on the inside.

Develop Spiritual Disciplines. We can use spiritual disciplines as a means of bringing congruency between our inner person and outer obedience. Throughout church history certain practices have been employed as aids to spiritual growth. These practices (or disciplines) are viewed from different perspectives.

Richard Foster's widely used book on spiritual growth, *Celebration of Discipline*, views them as "inward disciplines," "outward disciplines," and "corporate disciplines."[3]

> Inward disciplines are *meditation, prayer, fasting, study.*
> Outward disciplines are *simplicity, solitude, submission, service.*
> Corporate disciplines are *confession, worship, guidance, celebration.*

In his seminal study of how God changes lives, Dallas Willard advocates viewing the spiritual practices as "disciplines of abstinence" and "disciplines of engagement."[4]

> Disciplines of abstinence are *solitude, silence, fasting, frugality, chastity, secrecy, sacrifice.*

> Disciplines of engagement are *study, worship, celebration, service, prayer, fellowship, confession, submission.*

However we may characterize them, please read Willard's following explanation carefully. He maintains that the spiritual disciplines are the

> indirect means that allow us to cooperate in reshaping the personality—the feelings, ideas, mental processes and images, and the deep readiness of soul and body—so that our whole being is poised to go with the movements of the regenerate heart that is in us by the impact of the Gospel Word under the direction and energizing of the Holy Spirit.[5]

I concur with his statement because I saw this reshaping of the personality in my early experience of shoplifting and stealing. I meditated upon the Word of God and then realigned my thoughts, attitudes, and actions so as to live out the new, higher values that I had adopted. As I did so, I witnessed the Spirit's work of regeneration, transforming me from within, which in turn moved to transform my outward life. This transformation is itself dependent upon three larger factors, or conditions, of growth.

Conditions for Growth in Christ

The crux of biblical discipleship—that is, of forming the spirit of the believer—lies in the balance between *God's operation* in the disciple's life and the *disciple's response in obedience to God's operation.* The *attitude*, then, is all important.

If we want to grow in Christ, a proper attitude is a fundamental condition of the heart. A legalistic attitude can turn each of the disciplines into a negative experience. We can twist any spiritual practice into a means of measuring others' spirituality or of measuring our own. It is possible to be involved in these disciplines solely to impress others, or to relieve our spiritual guilt, without their affecting our internal life at all. That was the problem with the Pharisees. They could point to many disciplines and say that they were doing well. But they were performing them with a wrong motive and with a wrong perspective on true spirituality.

Therefore, as we go through this study and as we apply these truths throughout our lives, keep in mind that our transformation is dependent upon balancing three influences that bring growth:

- The example of Jesus (Luke 6:40, Romans 8:29, 1 Corinthians 11:1)
- The work of the Spirit (John 14:12-17)
- The obedience of the Christian (John 15:5)

Each of these factors is essential and the three must operate together. Consider what happens if only two of the three are at work without the balancing of the third.

What would happen if a Christian was strictly obedient to the example of Jesus but carried out that obedience in his or her own efforts, without the empowering of the Spirit? Such efforts can produce *legalism.* We know too well how futile it is to attempt to become like Jesus in our own efforts. The Spirit produces true growth.

What would happen if a Christian sincerely desired to be obedient and attempted to rely on the power of the Holy Spirit but did not look to the example of Jesus? Such an effort can produce *subjectivism,* that is, choosing what parts of God's Word we will obey based on individual whim. This is a danger with some who are enthusiastic about the ministry of the Spirit but who are not fully grounded in the Word of God. This is often a characteristic of a cult, when the cult leader substitutes himself or herself for the example of Jesus.

And what would happen to the Christian who studied diligently the example of Jesus and sincerely believed in the work of the Holy Spirit, but who never was obedient with his or her life and actions? Without obedience *nothing of spiritual value* is produced in the life of the believer. This is a hazard for the person who is diligent to study the Bible but who is not as diligent in applying it. None of these imbalances needs to be true of us.

The "Nonnegotiables" of Biblical Discipleship

We are now poised to enter into our study of the essential characteristics of biblical discipleship. In the next section, chapters five through ten, we will examine them one by one. In the third section, chapters eleven through thirteen, we will suggest some ways in which they can be lived out in a practical manner in our everyday world.

As we examine these characteristics of biblical discipleship, keep in mind that each is rooted in clear biblical teaching. And although we examine them individually, they contribute to the growth of the truly whole person, and by that I mean the disciple of Jesus who is in the process of becoming like Him.

Nonnegotiable biblical discipleship

- is grounded in a personal, costly relationship with Jesus;
- results in a new identity in Jesus;
- is guided by God's Word;
- is empowered by the Holy Spirit;
- is developed through a whole-life process;
- is practiced in communities of faith; and
- is carried out in our everyday world.

As we now move to examine and apply each one of these truths, I want to challenge you to develop a biblically based concept of discipleship. Let God's Word define what it means to grow in a life lived with Jesus. For God, and not programs or external standards of performance, is the author and finisher of our faith. He alone promises to direct our steps in a life of obedience.

I think often of those young surfers and volleyball players. Our only program was to love them unconditionally in Christ. And to this day, we are still here to help in the process. Just yesterday one of them came to us for help. Her brother had just collapsed and died of a brain aneurysm. She held onto us and cried. She hasn't yet become a Christian, but she knows that she can come anytime for help because she knows we love her as Jesus would if He were tangibly here now. We trust God that we are giving her and others an example of how their lives can also be transformed through a personal relationship with Him.

We are waiting and praying for the day when God's love and His offer of new life will penetrate to the core of her being, waiting for the day when she will let go of her old way of living—independently doing her own thing without God—and slip her hand into the hand of Christ.

Isn't that really what discipleship is all about?

■ PART TWO ■

WHAT DOES IT TAKE TO BECOME LIKE JESUS?

■

CHAPTER FIVE

A Personal, Costly Relationship with a Seeking Savior

The Lord Jesus Christ, the God-man,
is both a manifestation of divine love in us
and an example of human humility among us,
so that our great pride might be healed
by an even greater contrary medicine.
For a proud man is a great misery; but a
humble God is a greater mercy.

AUGUSTINE OF HIPPO,
RUDIMENTARY CATECHESIS (CIRCA A.D. 400)[1]

■

Several years ago while on a study tour in Israel, I met three fascinating Palestinian boys of about sixteen, all of whom had recently become Christians. As they introduced our group to various cultural traditions of the Middle East their eyes sparkled with excitement. But when we asked how their families had reacted to their conversions to Christ they became grave.

One said he'd been rejected by his family because he'd become a Christian. Another was living in the streets because his family had disowned him. The third had not yet dared to tell his family that he had become a Christian because they belonged to a fundamentalist Islamic sect. If his conversion became known, it would be his eldest brother's responsibility to kill him. He knew that the day would soon come when he could no longer keep his faith secret. And unless he could escape, it would then be a matter of having chosen eternal life over earthly life.

These young men had counted the cost of family allegiance against allegiance to Jesus. Their decision to receive Christ as Savior was by faith—and it was a costly faith.

Becoming a disciple of Jesus is always costly. It cost Jesus. And although it is nothing we can buy, it is costly for us, too. The cost is *life*.

Jesus, our Master, set the example for us when He came from heaven to give His life for us. He came seeking the spiritually ill to make them well and fit for His kingdom. This initiative was accomplished through the penalty He paid for our sins in His loving act of redemption on the cross. He gave His life so that we might have life (1 Corinthians 6:19-20). Jesus said, "For even the Son of Man did not come to be served, but to serve, and to give his life as a ransom for many" (Mark 10:45). Throughout His life He set His face toward the cross.

Likewise, the cost for us is life. While Jesus' death on the cross is unique, each of us must also lose our life and take up our own cross—that is, living in obedience to the life and work God would have us do. After telling His disciples that He was going to Jerusalem to die on the cross, Jesus said, "If anyone would come after me, he must deny himself and take up his cross and follow me. For whoever wants to save his life will lose it, but whoever loses his life for me will find it" (Matthew 16:24-25).

The Palestinian boys understood that cost. They realized that nothing else is of any value when compared to the gain of eternal life in Jesus Christ. So they sacrificed their families, their comforts, their standing and security and self-worth in the eyes of their own people, in order to enter into a relationship with Jesus.

What's most important for us to see from their example is that the cost involved more than just making a one-time choice. They had to consider the effect that choosing to follow Jesus would have on every single area of life. Whereas many of us in safe, comfortable environments choose Jesus for the future benefit of going to heaven and not to hell, or to help us overcome a personal problem so we can live a healthier and happier life, these young men and countless Christians like them have to continue to choose Christ every day as they live as persecuted minorities in religiously hostile environments. They wrestle every day with the temptation to go back to the easier way of life. The young Palestinians recognize every day that they do not have the same advantages and status as their Islamic friends. But every day that they sacrifice their old way of life—the acceptance and security and comfort others take for granted—they are brought into a deeper relationship with Jesus.

Jesus came to demonstrate what it means to live with your eyes on the high prize of abiding with God in daily service to Him. The cost we are asked to pay may not be demanded in such a dramatic way as it was from these Palestinian boys. But you and I are also asked to pay the cost of whole-hearted commitment to Christ. It is only through counting the cost and choosing Jesus that we enter eternal life. And it is through continuing to pay the cost of following Jesus that we live in touch with real, eternal life. So explore with me now what it means to have a costly relationship with Jesus.

Discipleship in the Ancient World

Jesus' form of discipleship stands out starkly when we compare it to other kinds of discipleship in the Middle East in His day. The term "disciple" was used generally to designate a follower who was committed to a recognized leader or teacher. When Jesus entered the scene of history in the first century, several other types of individuals were called "disciples." These disciples were similar to, yet quite different from, Jesus' disciples.

The Jews who questioned the parents of the man born blind (John 9:18) attempted to scorn the blind man by saying that, although he was a disciple of Jesus, they were "disciples of Moses" (John 9:28). They focused on their privilege of having been born Jews and that their special relation to God came through obedience to Moses' law (John 9:29).

The "disciples of the Pharisees" (Mark 2:18; Matthew 22:15-16) were adherents of the Pharisaic party, possibly belonging to one of their academic institutions. The Pharisees centered their lives on painstaking study and strict application of the Old Testament, developing a complex system of oral interpretations of the Law, in effect extending the law to every single activity of life.

The "disciples of John the Baptist" (John 1:35; Mark 2:18) were courageous men and women who had left the status quo of institutional Judaism to follow the prophet. Originally, Jesus' first disciples had been disciples of John (John 1:37), and John's and Jesus' disciples had similar activities in the early stages of Jesus' public ministry (John 3:22-24; 4:1-3).

Religious activity, study, following a baptizing prophet—these are characteristics of other forms of discipleship found in Israel. What was different about being a disciple of Jesus? It is this: Discipleship began then, and begins today, as a personal, costly relationship with the Master who came to seek us out. This is foundational.

Jesus Takes a Costly Initiative

Jesus lived in stark contrast to other religious leaders of His day because He came to bring spiritual healing to anyone who would confess his or her own spiritual illness—male or female, young or old, religiously pure or impure. Once a person accepted the offer of forgiveness and made a commitment of faith to follow Jesus, he or she became a disciple of Jesus. His offer of salvation to sinners based on faith in God's mercy and not based on observing religious traditions was a threat to the foundation and way of life of some groups like the Pharisees. So the love of God, which beats at the heart of the gospel He came to announce, left no room for *self*-righteousness. In the kingdom of God, He said, those who are spiritually healthy in their own eyes are like the blind leading the blind. Jesus said on the occasion of calling Matthew the tax-collector to salvation, "It is not the healthy who need a doctor, but the sick. But go and learn what this means: 'I desire mercy, not sacrifice.' For I [Jesus] have not come to call the righteous, but sinners" (Matthew 9:12-13).

Discipleship to Jesus began, not with the would-be disciple, but with Jesus. Jesus took the initiative to seek those in need and call them to follow Him. He offered healing for their souls through reconciliation with God. And the eternal irony of Jesus' initiative in seeking us out is that it came at a high cost to Himself—His own life.

And there was another, more important piece of Jesus' kind of discipleship.

When Jesus walked into a person's everyday world and extended His call to salvation, He asked that a response be made. That response was the pivotal point of the person's life. From that point he or she was a disciple or else that person turned away from Jesus. It was an either/or situation, because Jesus said that "He who is not with me is against me" (Luke 11:23). Once the response was made it marked the beginning of a new life and it meant continuing to choose to give up your old life (Matthew 8:34-37; Luke 9:23-25). It meant finding new life as an adopted child of God through obeying the will of the Father (Matthew 12:46-50).

What was the response that Jesus really looked for?

It is found in one of the most forceful passages in the Bible, in Luke's Gospel (Luke 14:25-35).[2] Large crowds of people were following Jesus around the countryside. They were curious about Him, but they had not yet made a faith commitment to Him. Jesus called them to become His disciples by issuing a threefold challenge:

> "If anyone comes to me and does not hate his father and mother, his wife and children, his brothers and sisters—yes,

even his own life—he cannot be my disciple." (verse 26)

"And anyone who does not carry his cross and follow me cannot be my disciple." (verse 27)

"Any of you who does not give up everything he has cannot be my disciple." (verse 33)

In any crowd of people one can find a mixture of priorities which drives individual lives. As Jesus looked at this crowd, He was calling individuals to salvation. In order to claim the salvation He offered, each person was faced with the choice to exchange the god of his or her life with Jesus as the true God of life. The cost varied from person to person, according to the god of each person's life, but the choice had to be made if one was to become Jesus' disciple.

He does the same with us. Choosing Him and the life He offers is the first step for the person who has not yet become a Christian, and it is also a daily challenge to each of us in our growth as His disciples.

Today, Jesus is still calling you and me to be honest about what it is that rules our lives. It could be a drug addiction, or it could be a boyfriend. It could be the pursuit of a Ph.D., the acceptance and respect of peers, or it could be an insatiable need for pleasure or the toys of life. The joys and securities and comforts these pursuits temporarily offer may not appear to be bad, but serving self is the real motive behind these types of choices. Jesus asks, "Is this ruler of your life keeping you from Me?"

So what does rule your life? What is it that must be dethroned because it is keeping you from experiencing freedom and fullness of life? Jesus calls you and me to come and follow Him so that He can save us from our old ways of life and offer us a new way of life. Examine yourself carefully now as we look at these three challenges.

The Cost of Family. The first challenge Jesus issued was toward those whose family relationships held the highest priority, and in a tribal culture family bonds were incredibly strong. Following Jesus meant putting Him in such a place of prominence that if any other commitment tried to usurp His place, one had to forcefully go against it. Nothing else was to substitute for Jesus as the focus of allegiance.

One of the young girls who was part of our surfer group became active in our local church and made a profession of faith in Jesus. But her mother, a Jehovah's Witness, soon made life difficult. She made her daughter feel guilty, insisting that she was rejecting her own mother by choosing Christianity. Finally the girl succumbed to the pressure and left the church to become active in the Jehovah's Witnesses with her mother. This young girl counted the cost of allegiance to her family against allegiance to Jesus and, at least for now, chose to stop following Jesus.

Because these choices have eternal consequences, Jesus insisted we must "hate" anything that commands allegiance above Him. This cannot mean literal, vicious hatred, because Jesus commanded His followers to love even their enemies (Luke 6:27). Rather, "hate" here means something like loving less (Genesis 29:31,33; Deuteronomy 21:15). Again, it indicates that we are to love God so preeminently that all other love relationships pale in comparison. And it points to the separation that must come when loyalties to anything in this world attempt to keep a person from following Jesus (Luke 8:20-21, 9:59-62). It also points to the necessity of subordinating everything, even one's own being, to one's commitment to Jesus (Luke 9:59-62, 16:13).

Jesus supported biblical family relationships, yet nothing must stand in the way of following Him to eternal life. Jesus did not call for a disruption of the family or rebellion against it. Rather, He declared that *He* must be the primary focus of allegiance.

The Cost of Self. Jesus pressed the point to those who had other competing allegiances. He said that anyone who does not take up his or her cross and follow Him cannot be His disciple. The full principle is given in the saying found earlier in Luke's gospel.

> "If anyone would come after me, he must deny himself and take up his cross daily and follow me. For whoever wants to save his life will lose it, but whoever loses his life for me will save it. What good is it for a man to gain the whole world, and yet lose or forfeit his very self? If anyone is ashamed of me and my words, the Son of Man will be ashamed of him when he comes in his glory and in the glory of the Father and of the holy angels." (Luke 9:23-26)

What is the *cross* that you must bear? Immediately, you might think of the difficulties that you have to endure in this life. But the expression, "take up your cross," must be understood in the context of

Jesus' prediction that He was going to the cross to die. The cross, while a terrible symbol of suffering and shame, was part of the Father's will for Jesus' life. Going to the cross was the purpose for which Jesus came to earth so that you and I might have eternal life. In the garden prior to the crucifixion, Jesus affirmed to the Father His willingness to go to the cross. Although He did not want to experience the physical torture of the crucifixion, He finally cried out, "not my will but yours be done" (Luke 22:42).

When understood in this way, the cross stands for much more than the daily difficulties we must endure. To take up your cross means to find and do God's will for your life day by day. It means to deny your own self-centered will for your life, embrace the Father's will, and follow Jesus as an outward demonstration of inner willingness to obey, no matter what the cost.

Who is your God? Whose will for your life do you follow? One of my students, a young woman who is confined to a wheelchair, has difficulties far more obvious and trying than mine. But her wheelchair is, in a way, only a barrier to taking up her cross. Her true cross is God's will for her life. She believes that God has called her to attend a Christian university so that she can train to be an elementary school teacher. So she has forsaken other goals, and every day she works to overcome the drawbacks of life in a wheelchair, to embrace God's calling on her life. And if you ask why she has such a gracious smile on her face, she will tell you it's because she knows God has a purpose for her life—to make a difference in the lives of the young people she will someday teach. Obedience to this mission is her cross. In her daily obedience to that calling, no matter what hardships come her way, she is following Jesus' example. The writer to the Hebrews said, "Let us fix our eyes on Jesus, the author and perfecter of our faith, who for the joy set before him endured the cross" (Hebrews 12:2). The joy of doing God's will, living the life we were created to live, is our goal.

The Cost of Everything. The final challenge of discipleship is given in Luke 14:33: "In the same way, any of you who does not give up everything he has cannot be my disciple." Here, Jesus is not calling for poverty as a means of obtaining salvation. But He knew that wealth and possessions are a god for most people. Jesus calls each one of us to find our security, self-worth, and power in Him. Too often our possessions, our profession, or our pleasures become our source of security, self-worth, or personal power. Nothing must be a substitute for God as the source of our soul's well-being, security, and power. Entrance into Jesus' way of discipleship means entering the narrow gate to salvation (Luke 9:23, 13:22-30).

Christians throughout the ages have had to pay the cost of surrendering their earthly pleasures and securities to follow Jesus alone, for the gods of materialism and pleasure-seeking are not new. Augustine, one of the theological giants of church history, was similarly held captive by these gods. After his conversion he wrote:

> The very toys of toys and vanities of vanities, my ancient mistresses, still held me; they plucked my fleshy garment, and whispered softly, "Will you cast us off forever? and from that moment shall we no longer be with you forever?"
>
> I hesitated to burst and shake myself free from them, for a violent habit said to me, "Do you really think you can live without them?"

But as the Spirit prompted Augustine to read Paul's words to the Romans, he was set free from their power over his life:

> I seized, opened, and in long silence read that section on which my eyes first fell: "Not in rioting and drunkenness, not in chambering and wantonness, not in strife and envying; but put on the Lord Jesus Christ, and make no provision for the flesh, to fulfill its lusts."
>
> No further would I read; nor needed I: for instantly at the end of this sentence, by a light as it were of serenity infused into my heart, all the darkness of doubt vanished away.[3]

Like many today, Augustine struggled with philosophical doubts about the truth of Christianity and with his own moral depravity. Historian Will Durant says of Augustine's conversion, "Surrendering the skepticism of the intellect, he found, for the first time in his life, moral stimulus and mental peace."[4] As he gave up the pleasure gods that ruled his life and allowed Jesus to rule his life, Augustine discovered eternal peace and a reality he had never before known.

This Cost Is . . . Your Life. Discipleship to Jesus begins with a divine paradox: We must die in order to live. The gods that rule our life must be sacrificed so that Jesus can be our God and Savior and Master.

One of the clearest ways of seeing this is in a person who rejected Jesus' offer of salvation. A rich young man once came to Jesus and asked, "Teacher, what good thing must I do to get eternal life?" (Matthew 19:16). Jesus knew the heart of this young man. He was devout and very serious about obeying the commandments of the Old Testament. But his real faith—his security and identity—was in his wealth.

Jesus challenged his god. He said, "If you want to be perfect, go, sell your possessions and give to the poor, and you will have treasure in heaven. Then come, follow me." But when the young man heard what Jesus required of him, "he went away sad, because he had great wealth" (Matthew 19:21).

Giving up his wealth would not have *earned* him salvation. Rather, Jesus was trying to help him see that the real god of his life—the thing that ruled all his choices—was his wealth. His only hope to enter the kingdom of God was to surrender the thing that governed him and accept a new ruler. Only under the rule of God can we be changed into true sons and daughters of God, directed by His Word and His Spirit so that we begin to fulfill His will on earth. And each one of us is called to surrender the old gods of our lives so that this surrendered-to-God attitude so perfectly demonstrated by Jesus is the attitude of our hearts, too. Then, in spirit, we are imitating Jesus.

C. S. Lewis clearly recognized what Jesus' challenge to count the cost of living in relationship with Him meant. He saw that we are called to place our lives into Jesus' hands so that He can perform the task of transforming us completely into His image. Lewis explains this powerfully from Jesus' standpoint.

> That is why He warned people to "count the cost" before becoming Christians. "Make no mistake," He says, "if you let Me, I will make you perfect. The moment you put yourself in My hands, that is what you are in for. Nothing less, or other, than that. You have free will, and if you choose, you can push Me away. But if you do not push Me away, understand that I am going to see this job through. Whatever suffering it may cost you in your earthly life, whatever inconceivable purification it may cost you after death, whatever it costs Me, I will

> never rest, nor let you rest, until you are literally perfect—until my Father can say without reservation that He is well pleased with you, as He said He was well pleased with Me. This I can do and will do. But I will not do anything less."[5]

Being a disciple of Jesus is for those who have counted the cost and want real life, eternal life, with a Savior who came to earth to seek and to save us, One who will lovingly, persistently transform us into His image.

These are tough words if you fear and resist Him. And words of hope, promise, peace, and joy if you are tired of ruling your life yourself.

How about you?

CHAPTER SIX

A NEW IDENTITY IN JESUS

The Father is well pleased with all the deeds that
Jesus has done for our salvation; and therefore
we are his, not only through our redemption
but also by his Father's courteous gift.
We are his bliss, we are his reward,
we are his honor, we are his crown.

JULIAN OF NORWICH,
REVELATIONS OF DIVINE LOVE (CIRCA A.D. 1373)[1]

■

Some of us can look back to a crisis event that permanently altered the direction of our lives. Psychologist John Trent calls these crisis events in our lives "flashpoints."[2]

A series of flashpoints impacted my life during my late teens and early twenties. One in particular created a genuine identity crisis.

I returned home in late 1969 from a tour of duty with the Army in Vietnam. My duty station back in the States was with the 82nd Airborne Infantry Division at Fort Bragg, North Carolina. My brother Bill was also stationed there, so I was able to stay with him and his wife for my last months in the service.

My experience fighting in the war in Vietnam had left me a very confused and troubled young man. I was troubled emotionally, intellectually, and spiritually. God had begun to work on my heart while I was in Vietnam, forcing me to look at my own emptiness and self-centeredness, and the emptiness of human solutions to depravity. I had not yet heard the gospel message about Jesus and was looking desperately for help.

My search led me to a variety of books on philosophy, religion, and pop-psychology. I got some help, but I also read a lot of junk which contributed to even more confusion.

I became a music freak and lay for hours listening to my stereo as various acid-rock groups wailed about their questions and tried to give answers to life. The deaths of Jimi Hendrix and Janis Joplin were devastating to me. If they ended *their* lives in futility, what hope was there for *me*?

Briefly, I turned to so-called "mind expanding" drugs, trying to find answers. These drugs were a tool of Satan and even from the first day they began to destroy my life. Nonetheless, God broke through to me.

Bill and I had dropped LSD. As I sat in an overstuffed chair allowing the drug to take me over, I began to ask questions about the direction of my life. Vividly, frighteningly, I imagined myself crawling out of my body and standing looking back at myself sitting in the chair. I felt a shock as I looked back at myself because there was no real Mike Wilkins. I was an empty shell—a combination of phony facades and games.

I really didn't know who I was. After I returned from Vietnam I was seen by my friends and family as a war hero. I was an airborne infantry sergeant to the troops for whom I was responsible. Yet when I was off post I played the role of a hippie. I portrayed myself as a person of the drug culture. I switched roles daily and even several times in one day. I played identity games with everyone I met in order to use them to get what I wanted.

And in that moment as I looked at myself, it was as though I died. I saw the dead emptiness in the core of my soul.

My brother Bill told me later that he came over to me while I was sitting in the chair and shook me, asking me what was wrong. He told me that I looked up at him and said, "Bill, I just died." Then I slumped over and stayed out of touch for the next several hours. It completely "bummed" his entire day until I came out of it!

From that time on I was never again able to do even the mildest drug without experiencing a paralyzing paranoiac knowledge that I was nothing.

In no way am I condoning drug use. But our infinitely merciful God used that incident to scare me about reality, and I was pushed to try to find out who I was.

Within a few weeks of the drug incident my enlistment time was over, and I returned home to California to go back to college. God was doing miraculous things on college campuses then, and soon I was gently and lovingly exposed to the message about life in Jesus. That message exploded my world! This was the *real* revolutionary answer to the questions I had been asking! Jesus was the undeniable God—and He came to earth to give us the truth about life, about who we really were as humans, and what our existence was supposed to mean.

When I looked into the face and life of Jesus, I saw my Savior and God. And in the light of Jesus' identity I began to see my own identity revealed. I was, quite simply, a person whom God loved. That might sound like a cliché, but to this day I can still recall how His love penetrated to the depths of my heart, like a voice saying, "Mike, I love you exactly the way you are. Let Me now help you to understand who you are and what I can make of your life."

As Trent says, it is the crisis incidents of our lives that teach us the truth about ourselves. Seeing my spiritual deadness in comparison to Jesus' light and life forever altered the direction my life story would take.

We also see flashpoints in the lives of many biblical characters. One who is especially transparent is Simon Peter. In an important encounter with Jesus, Peter was compelled to see himself and his entire life from an altogether new perspective. He began the process of transformation because of this encounter. On the outside he was still Peter, but inwardly he began to develop a new identity in relationship to Jesus.

It is important for us to look at this incident closely because we need to grasp how the process of becoming like Jesus transplants in us a new identity.

Jesus' Identity Tranforms Us

The incident I'm referring to is the miraculous catch of fish recorded in Luke 5:1-11. One day Jesus was teaching such a large crowd of people that He was forced to get into a boat and teach from the water. The boat belonged to Simon Peter. After He finished teaching, Jesus asked Peter to go out into the deep water to catch some fish.

Peter was most likely a successful fisherman. He and Andrew were in a fishing partnership with James and John (verse 10). They had been fishing all night but hadn't caught anything. Now Jesus wanted him to try again. I can imagine what was going through Peter's mind, (the expert fisherman), "Jesus, you may be a great teacher, but you don't know anything about fishing! But I'll humor you and drop my nets again."

Suddenly, violently, the nets were filled with such a large number of fish that they began to break. So they signaled their partners in the other boat to come and help, but the catch was so huge *both* boats began to sink (Luke 5:6-7).

From all accounts, Peter had been following Jesus for some time, perhaps upwards of a year. Andrew, Peter's brother, had originally introduced him to Jesus, saying, "We have found the Messiah." Peter had then become one of Jesus' first followers (John 1:35-42). We are not certain what kind of Messiah Andrew and Peter thought Jesus to be, perhaps a powerful military liberator sent from God to drive out the Romans.

Now, however, Peter saw clearly that Jesus was not simply a great teacher or prophet or military liberator: *Jesus was Lord* (Luke 5:8). Do not miss the important point: As Jesus' identity was more clearly revealed in Peter's mind and experience, *Peter's identity began to be transformed.* Consider what happened.

When Peter saw Jesus more clearly, he knew he was standing before the Holy One, which provoked a deeply felt confession. "When Simon Peter saw this, he fell at Jesus' knees and said, 'Go away from me, Lord; I am a sinful man!'" (Luke 5:8).

This is a most important beginning point. And from this beginning Jesus wanted to move Peter along. He did not leave him with the identity of *sinner*, though that humbling is a crucial first step. Instead He enlisted Peter as a *partner* in the ministry of seeking lost souls. "Then Jesus said to Simon, 'Don't be afraid; from now on you will catch men'" (Luke 5:10). This marked a radical reevaluation of Peter's own self-understanding and future because from that moment "they pulled their boats up on shore, left everything and followed him" (Luke 5:11).

As with Peter, we too must go through an interior upheaval and receive a new identity when we come into relationship with Jesus. In the light of Jesus' power and goodness, Peter could only see himself as a sinner, even though he had been a religious man. But in Jesus' eyes Peter was a new person. A transformation had begun even though Peter would allow his own self-centeredness to take over so that he opposed and even abandoned Jesus. The real source of the transformation came from the way Jesus viewed Peter—as a new man, a fisher of men, and a rock.

You and I can be so overwhelmed with our personal sins and failures, or with our deep hateful thoughts and vile imaginations, that we see ourselves only as sinners. But God views us differently. God views us as His beloved children, spiritually reborn into a new identity (John 1:12-13). The process has begun, and He will not let us remain the same. From God's perspective we are changed people, new creatures in Christ (2 Corinthians 5:17).

It is vitally important for us to see ourselves from that perspective. The starting point of transformation is the recognition that we are God's children. That is the starting point for everything we will become: the roles that we will carry out in life, the hurts and the failures that we will overcome, the accomplishments that we will achieve.

Some Christians get stuck in their awareness of sin, so they live feeling weak, defective, and ashamed—"sinners saved by grace" as the expression goes. But Paul never wrote his letters to "sinners." He wrote to the "saints" (Romans 1:7, 1 Corinthians 1:2, Philippians 1:1). From Paul's perspective a saint was not an elite category of Christians. A saint is a person whom God has set apart from all the other creatures in this world to love as His child. When we choose to follow Christ, that is the normal way God views us.

Toward the end of his life Peter impressed this point upon the new believers to whom he writes a forceful letter of encouragement. He wrote,

> For you have been born again, not of perishable seed, but of imperishable, through the living and enduring word of God. . . . You are a chosen people, a royal priesthood, a holy nation, a people belonging to God, that you may declare the praises of him who called you out of darkness into his wonderful light. (1 Peter 1:23, 2:9)

What an incredibly powerful way of seeing ourselves—"a chosen people, a royal priesthood, a holy nation, a people belonging to God"!

Why am I emphasizing this point? Because the way we view ourselves affects the way we live out our lives *and* the way we treat other people.

I knew a wonderful older pastor who had retired from ministry. He had a form of painful, crippling arthritis that contorted his limbs. And yet I never saw him without a smile. In spite of his own suffering he was our visitation pastor, going into the home of every visitor to our church, going into the hospital room of every person who was sick. He was a wonderful example to me of a pastor with a servant's heart. Once, while sharing a devotional reflection on the cross of Christ, he said: "I am not *worthy* of Christ's sacrifice on the cross, but I am of such *worth* to him that he died for me."

Because he knew his own value in God's eyes, he embodied love and compassion and care for the sick and the lost.

The Way I Relate to God

When I entered into my relationship with Jesus I also experienced a complete alteration of the way I related to God. Up to that point He had been an unknown being, a distant hope and threat. Then I began to understand that the Father loves me as His child, no matter what happens.

During our daughter Wendy's senior year in high school, she had a curfew of midnight. One Saturday night, Lynne woke up at 1:15 A.M. and Wendy was not home. Because Wendy was almost never late coming in at night, Lynne woke me. We paced the floor, becoming increasingly distraught. At 2:00 A.M., as I was about to call the police, Wendy drove up the driveway.

She told us that she got involved helping one of her friends who was having boyfriend problems. She knew she was late but didn't want to call and wake us.

The rush of emotions we experienced! We were so relieved she was safe, yet we were so upset with her irresponsible behavior.

In spite of any consequences she faced, I wanted Wendy to know that we love her. I am her father, and nothing she can do will change our relationship. I may be upset with her. I may have to discipline her. But I will always love her as her father. When she knows that about herself, it will affect everything she does.

The way you relate to God also affects dramatically the way that you approach life. If God is only your *taskmaster* then you will feel that the Christian life, your relationship with Him, is a burden. If God is a *disciplinarian* then you will cringe when you err or become devious to try to avoid His anger. But if you first and foremost view your heavenly Father as *one who loves you* and wants to nurture you and guide you through life, then you know that the tasks and the discipline are for your own good.

The Way I Relate to Others

Once we take hold of our worth to God and His care for us, our new identity in Christ will affect the way that we relate to others.

Jesus' summons is an act of grace, calling unworthy sinners to follow Him. But once we respond, we are part of one family, equals. The boundaries that divide us are broken down.

Reconciling us with each other was an essential part of Jesus' ministry. He broke through the barriers which separated the clean and unclean, the obedient and sinful. He summoned the fisherman, the tax collector and the zealot. Jesus called to Himself those who, in the eyes of sectarians like the Pharisees, did not seem to have the necessary qualifications for fellowship with Him (Matthew 9:9-13, Mark 2:13-17). In calling the despised to Himself, in eating with publicans, in restoring a fallen Samaritan woman, Jesus demonstrated that each could answer a call to fellowship with God *and* have fellowship with each other.

Developing Our Identity in Christ

When I became a Christian, Jesus began the process of developing my new identity. After about ten years I could look back and see five definite steps, or stages, He took me through in the process of developing a new identity in Christ.

They are:

Know Yourself (Psalm 139:13-14). The beginning point of developing our new identity in Christ is to know who we are as God has created us. Notice that I have placed two columns below.

	GOOD	BAD
1.		
2.		
3.		
4.		
5.		
6.		
7.		
8.		
9.		
10.		

In the left column write out ten good things about yourself. These can be physical characteristics, or personality characteristics, or emotions, or mental capabilities. This is the time for you to appreciate the way God has made you. If you are intelligent, or if you have good athletic abilities, or if you have a special love for people, list these things. God has created each of us with strengths, and we must be able to articulate what they are if we are to maximize their use in our lives. It is false humility to deny the strengths God has given us.

Once you have written out ten good things in the left column, list in the right column ten bad things about yourself. Think of ten things you just don't like about yourself. Again, these can be physical, emotional, mental, whatever. This is the time to write out those things that you know are bad, or that you don't like, or that cause you pain. You might write, "My personality when I'm with people." Or, "My ears are too big." Or, "I have a terrible temper."

Some of you may have no difficulty at all writing down your negative points because you have been cautioned your whole life to be humble. I certainly agree that humility is a major indicator of godliness, but listen to the psalmist David:

> For you created my inmost being;
>   you knit me together in my mother's womb.
> I praise you because I am fearfully and wonderfully made;
>   your works are wonderful,
>   I know that full well. (Psalm 139:13-14)

When was the last time you looked at yourself in the mirror and said, "I'm wonderful!"? How many of us can look at ourselves and say, "I am fearfully and wonderfully made"? We all should be able to say this because we each have been created in the image of God. King David knew only too well his own sinfulness and the personal weaknesses that wreaked tragedy for him and those around him. But he also knew the good in his own life that could be used to serve God.

God wants us to know fully who He created us to be. If we don't take the time to look carefully at ourselves objectively and come to know who we are, good and bad, we can't be effective in offering ourselves to God and others.

Accept Yourself from God's Perspective (Psalm 8:3-8). The second step is to accept yourself in the same way that God accepts you. He loves you right now. He knows who you are, both good and bad, and He still loves you. In fact, Paul tells us that "God demonstrates his own love for us in this: While we were still *sinners*, Christ died for us" (Romans 5:8, emphasis added).

David gives us a balanced perspective of who we are in Psalm 8. On the one hand he acknowledges that humans are not very significant when compared to the heavenly beings, the sun and stars. Yet, on the other hand, humanity is crowned with glory and honor and made the ruler over all of God's earthly creatures (Psalm 8:3-8).

Try to look at yourself and say, "OK, I have good and I have bad. Everyone has good and bad. I'm not going to get too hung up on either one. I will let God use the strengths and transform the weaknesses. I'll trust in His love and the transforming power of His Spirit, and I'll cooperate as He gives me the strength and wisdom to grow."

One deadly trap we must avoid is the trap of *comparing*. When we compare ourselves with others we are usually unrealistic—and someone *always* loses. If we have a poor self-image, when we compare our personal characteristics with other people's, we tend always to lose. If we think too highly of ourselves we tend to put other people down, and they lose. *Comparison robs us of the uniqueness that God has given to each of us.*

That's why you and I need to have a healthy acceptance of ourselves. We need to say, "I have good and bad. So does everyone else. A healthy acceptance of myself simply says that I have good and bad, and God loves me and wants to live His life in me. And I will let Him."

Build on the Good, Grow from the Bad (Romans 12:3). Once we have taken a good look at ourselves to know who we are and have then simply accepted who we are, we can then go on to the third step—building on our good points and growing from our weak areas.

Take a good look at your list of good and bad. Strategize on how to accomplish whatever God calls you to do by building on your strengths. I have discovered that I have a strength in the area of academics and teaching. I love to study and learn. I love to pass on to others what I have learned. So I build on my strengths in the area of teaching as God's calling on my life.

But I can't just look at the good. Paul says, "Do not think of yourself more highly than you ought, but rather think of yourself with sober judgment, in accordance with the measure of faith God has given you" (Romans 12:3).

I have strengths, but I also have weaknesses. I can only let God use and transform those parts of me as I face them realistically. I took a basic psychological test years ago when I was in seminary. The results indicated that along with some very positive traits, I had some extreme weaknesses: I was an extreme *loner*, I was extremely *angry*, and I was extremely *self-centered.* I basically didn't care about people, I didn't like people, and didn't know how to love people. I didn't trust anyone. I was a fairly new Christian at the time and I rationalized it all away. I avoided the results, hiding them from myself for about a year. Finally, one day I brought them out and showed them to Lynne. She looked at them carefully and then said emphatically, "Yes, that's you!"

I couldn't avoid my weaknesses any longer! Lynne and two of my friends at the seminary took me on as a project. Over the next two years they wouldn't leave me alone! They would sit with me in class and at chapel. They took me to lunch. And my wife gently but firmly taught me how to care about people.

That was over twenty years ago. After pastoring two churches and teaching for nearly fifteen years, caring about people is no longer a weakness. In fact, in the evaluations my students give me each semester, they consistently remark, "Dr. Wilkins doesn't just teach, he really cares about us." True, I have other weaknesses to be surrendered to Christ. But I have allowed God to build on my strengths and have let Him correct me in my weaknesses.

Look back once more at the lists of your good and bad points. Draw a star next to the areas that are your *greatest strengths*. Focus on them to help you maximize your life and your calling. Then place a cross next to your *weakest areas*. By committing all these areas to God, you can watch the miracle of transformation spread throughout your whole life.

Forget about Yourself (Luke 9:23). Now comes a crucial stage in the process of developing your identity in Christ. With the fourth step we make a major transition.

The first three steps are vitally important in caring for our needs and developing our uniqueness as God's children. In fact, they are essential.

But from one perspective they are not really unique to Christianity. They are essential starting points in our human development, and they can also be found in most secular self-help books. With step four we now make unique strides.

At this stage of the process we must begin to forget about ourselves. The essence of Jesus' statement about denying ourselves is this: *We are to deny our own self-centered will for our lives.*

Consider the first three steps. Who are we thinking about? Ourselves! The danger of much self-help, self-image teaching, and unfortunately some Christian teaching on self-image, is that it has become unbalanced in focusing on ourselves.

I want to say this kindly, but I have found that often the person who has the worst self-image is the most self-centered. Why? Because he hurts so much that the only one he can think about is himself. And that is quite natural. I rarely think about my little toe. But yesterday morning I was walking barefoot on the patio and ripped it open on a board. I gave more attention and care to that little toe for the next half-hour than it had ever received! And I've thought about it quite a bit in the last two days!

It is necessary to give adequate attention to our pain and our development. When we look back at the first three steps, our focus has been on ourselves. As we continue to grow throughout our lives we will return to them as we come to know about ourselves or when a particularly weak area causes us pain.

The truth is, we must continue to press on, for there is more. The Christian life is not only about my growth and development. That is not much different from my old life where my world was myself. If you and I are to find the purpose for our lives and the purpose for our developing identities we must look outside ourselves. Denying ourselves is not the *goal*, it is a *means* to the goal, which is found in the next stage of the process.

Get into God's People (Mark 10:45). Jesus described His mission by saying, "For even the Son of Man did not come to be served, but to serve, and to give his life as a ransom for many" (Mark 10:45).

Jesus gave His life as the unique, once-for-all ransom for humanity. But we can follow His broader example, nonetheless. As we surrender everything to God we are filled with His life-giving Spirit, and He helps us to meet every challenge of every day. And the more we rely on Him for strength, the less we wind up focusing on our own needs.

And so—at last!— we can get our eyes off ourselves and give ourselves to care for other people. We become Jesus' servants reaching out to people with care and with the hope of the gospel.

Self-forgetfulness makes it possible for me to be a joyful servant. That may sound terribly religious at first, but it gets at the essence of what it means to be truly human, caring about others and giving our lives to better the existence of people around us. When we arrive at this point we recognize that through the indwelling Spirit's work and the example of Jesus we have been introduced into true humanity through the new birth. We now are whole in the way God had designed us to be from the beginning of creation.

The Process of a Lifetime

Developing our identity in Christ is a process that occurs throughout our lives. Considering these five steps, where do you think you are right now in the process? How well do you:

1. Know yourself?
2. Accept yourself from God's perspective?
3. Build on the good, grow from the bad?
4. Forget about yourself?
5. Get into God's people?

Most of my students find themselves at the first or second stage of the process. They are asking the big questions about who they are, why they are here, and what they will do with their lives. By the time they graduate from college I hope that they are moving toward step five.

The truth is, throughout our lives, we move through these stages over and over. For we continue to discover things about ourselves we never knew, and we step into new roles that challenge our skills and character as never before.

How good it is to know that Jesus allows us to function as servants no matter where we are in the process of growth. And we can choose to live as servants to the best of our ability, no matter how close we are to the beginning of the path of life in Christ.

Help for the Long Haul

Let me conclude with two hints that have been helpful to me.

Live with the Truth about Yourself. When we know the truth about who we are, we are able to make that a daily, powerful source of freedom that allows us to live life the way God has designed it. Memorize pertinent passages of Scripture that help you to know who you are in Christ. Some of the first passages I memorized as a new Christian helped me to understand clearly my new identity.

- John 1:12 teaches us that *we are children of God.*
- Galatians 2:20 and 2 Corinthians 5:17 teach us that *we have new life in Christ.*
- Ephesians 2:10 tells us that *we are God's workmanship and workers.*
- 1 Corinthians 3:16 teaches us that *our bodies are the temple of God.*
- Romans 8:35 tells us that *nothing can separate us from the love of God.*
- 1 Corinthians 10:13 declares that *no temptation can overtake us because God is there with us to provide a way of standing firm.*
- 1 John 5:18 declares that *we are born of God and the evil one cannot touch us.*

Understand clearly the truth of who you are in Christ. As you live with the truth about your identity in Christ, the truth will set you free! (See John 8:31-32.)

Make Your New Identity a Matter of Public Record. Be sure that you make your new identity a matter of public record. One of the earliest practices of the early church was baptism. When a person was baptized, the entire community knew that this person had now become identified with Jesus.

Do people around you know that you are a Christian? What demonstrates your identity? When I was in Korea a couple of years ago, I was impressed by the vitality of the church there. Koreans who came out of a nonChristian background often took a biblical name to indicate that they were new persons in Christ.

How eager are you to make your identity in Jesus known? I don't have a fish on my car, I don't wear a cross, my denomination doesn't wear robes or a collar. But, in whatever ways are appropriate, I let my identity be known. I am pleased to belong to Jesus.

As you proceed along the path of becoming like Jesus, let your life and your words declare that you have taken His identity for your own. As we close this chapter, consider the words of the great American preacher, philosopher, and theologian, Jonathan Edwards:

> On January 12, 1723, I made a solemn dedication of myself to God, and wrote it down; giving up myself, and all that I had to God; to be for the future, in no respect, my own; to act as one that had no right to be himself, in any respect. And solemnly vowed to take God for my whole portion and felicity; looking on nothing else, as any part of my happiness, nor acting as if it were.[3]

Today, and every day, step into the will of God for you, which is to grow in your new identity in Jesus Christ.

CHAPTER SEVEN

INDIVIDUAL TRANSFORMATION THROUGH THE SPIRIT

If you be the children of God . . . consider that the holy God is your Father, and let this oblige you to live like the children of God, that you may look your Father in the face with comfort another day.

JOHN BUNYAN,
"THE NEW BIRTH" (A.D. 1688)[1]

■

I recently heard a student describe her businessman father rather sarcastically: "Oh, he has a life. Sure! All he does is work, eat, and sleep." She desperately wanted her father to enjoy a fullness of life. Life does not consist simply in biological activity. Life is more than simply eking out an existence.

I am most alive when I am properly connected to what is real. *Life involves connectedness with the fullness of reality.* The relationships with my wife and children, the enjoyment of creation on a summer morning hike in the mountains with friends—these things connect me to life in such a way that I am *more* alive.

And at the most foundational level—the spirit—to be alive requires a connectedness with spiritual reality. We are different from all other creatures because of the potential of connectedness with spiritual life. Paul's monumental description of men and women in a vital relationship with God is that we are "alive to God" (Romans 6:11). Apart from God, we are said to be *dead.* Not physically dead—yet—but walking-around dead. Paul tells us that when we were separate from Jesus, we were "dead in [our] transgressions and sins" (Ephesians 2:1).

God offers us the chance to experience life in all its dimensions. I am passionate about helping Christians become more effective at living life as God intended it to be lived—fully, robustly. The reason Jesus came to earth was to call us out of spiritual death into the fullness of life which is found in relationship with the God who *is* life. The apostle John will guide our steps in this chapter because he gives us the most straightforward description of the life that Jesus came to bring.[2]

From Death to Life

When we receive our new identity in Christ, one of our fundamental characteristics is that we have passed from death to life (John 5:24). As Jesus emphasized, a disciple is born to new life by the Spirit of God (John 3:5-8).

In one of His earliest recorded conversations, Jesus instructed Nicodemus about the need for new life (John 3:1-15). Nicodemus was one of the religious elite of Israel: he was a Pharisee, an expert in both the Old Testament and the oral traditions, and he was a member of the highest Jewish ruling council in Israel, the Sanhedrin. Jesus called him "Israel's teacher" (verse 10).

But for all his religious accomplishments, Nicodemus still was lacking something. He was lacking the spiritual life which accompanied Jesus' inauguration of the kingdom of God. In spite of Nicodemus' knowledge of the Law and his excellent life, Jesus declared to him, "I tell you the truth, no one can see the kingdom of God unless he is born again" (verse 3).

This phenomenon of new birth is spoken of variously by different New Testament authors: regeneration (Titus 3:5); new birth and born again (1 Peter 1:3, 23); spiritual resurrection (Romans 6:13; Ephesians 2:5); new creation (2 Corinthians 5:17; Ephesians 2:10); and having God's seed in us (1 John 3:9).

Collectively these statements are overwhelming. We are different persons once we are given new life by the Spirit. The supernatural work of God deep within our soul implants new spiritual life in us. This is an instantaneous event that happens only once in our lives. From that moment on, the direction of our lives is placed Godward as the Holy Spirit begins to produce new life—the life of Jesus, which was centered in God—in place of our old life, which was centered in our selfish desires.[3]

There is mystery involved in the process because this is the work of God in our inner lives. Some people are aware of the beginnings, especially people who come to Christ in adult life.

C.S. Lewis, who came to Christ in adulthood, tells of his own awakening,

> I know very well when, but hardly how, the final step was taken. I was driven to Whipsnade one sunny morning. When we set out I did not believe that Jesus Christ is the Son of God, and when we reached the zoo I did. Yet I had not exactly spent the journey in thought. Nor in great emotion.[4]

But many people who grow up in Christian homes are not always aware of the beginning. For many it comes in the natural course of their growth. They may have turned to God in a moment not connected with a crisis event, so the experience of the awakening is not remembered consciously. Their spiritual life was initiated by God more quietly in the secrecy of their inner person.

Regardless of our conscious experiences, our transformation into the image of Jesus begins as God implants spiritual life in our soul. Then we are awakened to, alive in, God.

What awaits us now is to see how it can be nurtured, and what it will do in and through us.

Spiritual Life Must Be Nurtured

The apostles John and Peter both insist that the new life which we possess in Christ results from the "seed of God" implanted in us. This seed—and we'll consider its nature in a moment—is the ruling force which assures our natural growth to be like Jesus. The renowned Cambridge scholar of the last century, Brooke Foss Westcott, comments:

> The principle of life which He has given continues to be the ruling principle of the believer's growth. God gives, as it were, of Himself to the Christian. He does not only work upon him and leave him. The germ of the new life is that out of which the mature man will in due time be developed.[5]

Jesus gave His life *for* us; then through the Spirit He gave His life *to* us. And the wonderful truth is that Jesus' life produces results in His people. These results, or evidences of spiritual life, are a special focus of Jesus' form of discipleship. John's gospel gives us the three primary characteristics of this inside-out, life transformation in Jesus' disciples:[6]

- *Freedom*: transformation of mind and will (John 8:31-32)
- *Love*: transformation of heart (John 13:34-35)
- *Fruit*: transformation of character (John 15:7-8)

These characteristics set Jesus' disciples apart from all others.

As we look at them now, we do so to understand the Spirit's labor of love in us, and to learn how to allow His work to transform our daily lives.

Freedom: Transformation of Mind and Will

The first characteristic of Jesus' disciples is that we are *free*. It is a freedom far richer than most of us realize.

Ask people on the street what it means to be free and they will normally say something like "the ability to choose between different options" or "the right and ability to make my own decisions and do what I want to do." Human beings take freedom seriously. Forced bondage goes against our grain. We say, "I want to do *my* thing."

There is another perspective on freedom, however, and it is unique to Jesus' disciples. It surfaces during a discussion between Jesus and some Jews who had become attached to Him:

> To the Jews who had believed him, Jesus said, "If you hold to my teaching, you are really my disciples. Then you will know the truth, and the truth will set you free."
>
> They answered him, "We are Abraham's descendants and have never been slaves of anyone. How can you say that we shall be set free?"
>
> Jesus replied, "I tell you the truth, everyone who sins is a slave to sin. Now a slave has no permanent place in the family, but a son belongs to it forever. So if the Son sets you free, you will be free indeed." (John 8:31-36)

Jesus was pointing these men to a much higher form of freedom than they'd ever imagined: True freedom comes when we are set free from sin. This is similar to what Paul says in Romans 6 when he says that our old self has been crucified with Christ. The result is that "we should no longer be slaves to sin—because anyone who has died has been freed from sin" (Romans 6:6-7).

From Jesus' perspective, freedom is the ability to do the right and good thing, the ability to choose God, to be set free from sin's bondage. Outside of a surrendered relationship to God, a relationship in which we look to Him for our innermost needs, we are chained by sin, the essence of which is self-centeredness and pride (see Romans 3:9-18). The new life Jesus gives His disciples frees them from self-centeredness and pride, and it enables them to rest in the presence of a loving Father who helps them consistently choose His way of living life.

Unfortunately, many believers have not been trained fully to accept and live in the truth about our new, empowering life. They are not trained to abide in, or hold on to, Jesus' teaching in a way that helps them open up to God and find real life.

It is Jesus' teaching, His Word, that gives us freedom from the lies of the deceiver and the ways of the world. The lie of Satan from the very beginning has been to trap us in religious works or good deeds or efforts to earn our salvation. His lies even trap many believers in vicious, joyless self-condemnation as they focus intently on cleaning up their lives by a supreme effort of their own will, apart from the inner strengthening of the Spirit. This is the way of many people, whether it is in religions, or in the cults, or in some extreme self-help groups.

For Jesus' disciples alone, there is an open way, a way to freedom from bondage to sin. And freedom to *live out* the truth of God and the ways of God. This is a distinct mark of discipleship to Jesus. Discipleship begins with claiming Jesus' teaching about eternal life as the only way to salvation; growth in discipleship comes by holding on to Jesus' teaching for *every* area of life.

The world will try to sell us on various lies about freedom by controlling various aspects of reality. Knowing the truth from Jesus about each area of life breaks the chains of sin, as we claim His view of reality—that God is the source of meaning, healing, supply, and freedom—as our own. Instead of valuing and trusting in what the world says, we value and trust in what Jesus says. And that inward exchange of values then works from the inside to the outside. As it becomes our governing value system of life, it affects the way we think, act, and relate to others.

For example, the world tells us we can be free from feeling inferior by becoming a success. What that means, of course, is success in this life and in the eyes of other people. So the world will try to sell us on money, power, prestige, fame, or professional accomplishment as the proofs of success.

But Jesus said that the ultimate statement of success comes at the end of our lives when our heavenly Father says to us, "Well done, good and faithful servant."

Growth in the image of Jesus occurs when we compare *the words and values of the world* with *the words and values of Jesus* and then *adopt His teachings as our standards for life*. This is precisely the directive of Jesus in the Great Commission, when new disciples are taught to obey everything Jesus commanded as their means of growth (Matthew 28:20).

Businessmen are confronted with this kind of decision daily, where the world's ways of getting ahead financially are often at odds with biblical values. For example, a man may be tempted secretly to substitute supplies or services that are of a slightly inferior quality than what the customer is paying for. The customer will probably never know the difference (so the man rationalizes), and the result is a higher profit. A contractor friend told me that when he began to live out the truths of the Word about such things as honesty, integrity, and servanthood to his customers (Ephesians 4:25-32 is his professional guideline), something radical happened. He was set free from subtle habits of lying, stealing, and deception. He was also set free from a nagging guilty conscience, and from a foreboding fear of getting caught and punished. He said that he was now able to walk around town, go to church, and look customers in the eye knowing that he had done the best work he possibly could. The feeling, he says, is exhilarating because now he isn't trapped by the temptation to make an extra, shady buck.

Think of your own situation and the temptations that accompany it. What can you do to develop a solid plan and pattern of life in which you learn the truth about life from God's perspective and then adopt it as your own value for every area of your life? We cannot be set free from the lies the world tells us until we know the truth from God.

As Jesus' disciples we receive and abide in Jesus' words and experience a transformation of mind and will. We are set free by the truth to live life to the fullest in the way God intended life to be lived.

Do You Want to Grow in Freedom?

There are three solid suggestions for growth as a disciple—a man or woman who is set free from the ways of the world to follow the ways of God.

Get God's Truth. Develop a habit of acquiring the Word of God.

When we interact with the Word of God it is a spiritual activity. Hebrews tells us that "The word of God is living and active. Sharper than any double-edged sword, it penetrates even to dividing soul and spirit, joints and marrow; it judges the thoughts and attitudes of the heart" (Hebrews 4:12). As we allow the teachings of God to penetrate our hearts about every area of our lives, they will alter our values, motives, and goals in life. Our entire person—physical, mental, emotional, social, spiritual—is set free to conform to the will and personality of God.

That is why disciplines—that is, practices meant to train us in spirit—are crucial. I am referring to disciplines such as study, meditation, worship, and guidance or spiritual direction. By practicing these disciplines we acquire God's truth about life and allow others to help us live them out. This is why it is important not only to be involved consistently in your own individual study but also to be in small groups and corporate gatherings. We not only acquire the teachings of the Word, but we can also be with other brothers and sisters who provide us with guidance and who hold us accountable to the truth. What commitment will you make to a regular acquisition of the truth of God's Word?

When Jesus says that "abiding in His word" will be a characteristic of His disciples, He does not mean perpetual Bible study or even that having a regular devotional time is an evidence of spirituality. It is possible to have a regular devotional time, or to be a Bible whiz, without actually growing as Jesus' disciple. (Remember the scribes and Pharisees of Jesus' day. They were the leading authorities of Old Testament Scripture, and yet many were spiritually lifeless.)

The practices of study, guidance, and Scripture meditation are the means to an end, that is, acquiring God's truth so that we can grow in His love and service like Jesus. They are not final goals themselves. God's Word is our soul's food, and we "eat to live, not live to eat." We feed upon the Word of God to gain spiritual nourishment to live each day. We can become fat Christians if we do not exercise by acting on God's Word.

If you do not do so already, start practicing spiritual disciplines that help you know yourself and God's Word. You can find solid introductions to the disciplines of study and meditation in resources such as Richard Foster's *Celebration of Discipline*, or Donald Whitney's *Spiritual Disciplines for the Christian Life*.[7]

Question the World. Make a regular practice of questioning the values and the teachings of the world.

Whenever you are engaged with any of our media—newspapers, television, magazines, film, radio—make it a practice to be *aware*. By that I mean be alert to the thinking of our culture and to the influences of its values upon your life and the lives of those for whom you are responsible. Too often, we are not active participants who engage the media with an appropriate criticism.

Also, be alert to the values of the day as you watch trends within the educational field and in the political agendas of local, national and international bodies, and in music and the arts.

You might call this the discipline of discernment. And in order to help you practice it well, I add a couple of warnings: (1) Be *cautiously* critical. Keep yourself from becoming a sponge that soaks up whatever comes your way. If you are a sponge you will be subtly influenced by values you do not desire. (2) Be *wisely* critical. Be balanced in your critique so that you are not overly negative or positive. Be prepared to acknowledge both the good and the bad you will find. Learn from both.

Cling to God's Truth. Finally, counteract the influences of the world by clinging to Jesus' teaching.

Now that you have listened to both, you are able to compare practically the words of the world with the words of Jesus. As you look at some of the issues I have listed below, use the following format:

1. Try to state clearly your understanding of the "words of the world," which are the values and teachings of the secular world.
2. State as clearly as possible, with verse references, your understanding of the "words of God." If the Bible does not speak directly to the issue, try to articulate related biblical principles that can help you understand God's will on an issue. Small groups are helpful here because you receive

input from others who may have knowledge or experience in similar issues. It also opens you up to others who can help you be accountable to live out the truth.

3. Resolve how you will begin to incorporate God's teaching into your personal life and in the lives of those for whom you are responsible. (I have included a section at the end of this chapter which asks some questions for you to resolve. These are offered as a beginning point to help you rethink and adjust your values.)

As Jesus' disciples, receive and abide in Jesus' words. In this way, you will experience transformation of mind and will. Wayne Grudem says:

> As we gain in true understanding of God, his Word, and his world, we begin to think more and more of the thoughts that God himself thinks. In this we are "renewed in knowledge" [Colossians 3:10] and we become more like God in our thinking. This is a description of the ordinary course of the Christian life.[8]

We are set free by the truth to live life to the fullest in the way God intended life to be lived.

Love: Transformation of Heart

The second major change that comes as we grow in our new life in Jesus is *love*. Receiving Jesus' love causes a transformation of heart by which we are able to love each other with God's love. During the last supper Jesus told His first disciples, "A new command I give you: Love one another. As I have loved you, so you must love one another. By this all men will know that you are my disciples, if you love one another" (John 13:34-35).

Love became a distinguishing mark of the early church. Even when the church experienced vicious persecution, the result was a fellowship of love. It was love that the world noticed—a selfless, joyful giving that the world had not seen before. Love showed the world that these people really were Jesus' disciples.

The early church father Tertullian wrote his *Apology* in A.D. 197, approximately a century-and-a-half after Jesus spoke these words. During a time of fierce persecution he pointed to Christians' love for each other as a testimony of the reality of the Christian faith. As the church cared for their own poor and orphans and imprisoned, the pagans of that day marveled at such concern for one another. Tertullian states:

> It is mainly the practice of such love that leads some to put a brand on us. "See," they say, "how these Christians love one another! . . . And how ready they are to die for one another!"[9]

The distinguishing characteristic of Jesus' disciples in any era is His love. How does Jesus' love come into and change our heart?

Through the new birth, Jesus' love for us changes the spiritual heart of the believer. By "spiritual heart" I mean the center of our spiritual and emotional and psychological life. The spiritual heart is, first, where I encounter God. It is also where I experience life's joys and sorrows, where I connect deeply with other persons, and where I ponder my existence. The transformation that occurs in our heart when we are born anew is miraculous.

The heart of the person who is not born anew is said to be "deceitful above all things and beyond cure. Who can understand it?" (Jeremiah 17:9). God's indictment against fallen humanity is that "every inclination of his heart is evil from childhood" (Genesis 8:21).

But through the new birth the Spirit of God gives us a new, pure heart through faith (Acts 15:9). The new covenant that Jesus brought fulfilled one of God's greatest promises: "I will give you a new heart and put a new spirit in you; I will remove from you your heart of stone and give you a heart of flesh" (Ezekiel 36:26).

As we open ourselves to Him, Jesus' love will make a radical transformation of our heart. You may have been hurt or used by others in the past who said that they love you. But their love was self-centered, and so they took from you what they could get. You could easily block yourself off from Jesus' love because of your fear of being hurt or used again. But Jesus' love is *giving*. He gave Himself to die for you. He gives His Spirit to heal you, to give you peace, to make you whole, to take away your fear. It is as you open your heart to trust in His kind of love that your inner person begins to be transformed.

As a result of knowing we are eternally loved, we come to love God. In our transformation we are able to love others because we have a new heart that impels us to love. I encourage you to ponder John's inspired wisdom on the interaction and potency of God's love in us:

> We love because he first loved us. If anyone says, "I love God," yet hates his brother, he is a liar. For anyone who does not love his brother, whom he has seen, cannot love God, whom he has not seen. And he has given us this command: Whoever loves God must also love his brother. (1 John 4:19-21)

We love because God first loved us and made a change in our hearts, and this dynamo of love now *impels* us to love.

God is love, and He is infinite, so He has an infinite supply of love. As we open our heart to Him, His love pours into our heart and then overflows to those around us. His endless supply of love is available to us to give to others.

Do you realize what this means? It means that as regenerate people we have a new heart which will love. And we are connected spirit to Spirit with an endless supply of love from God by which we can continually pour forth love (1 John 4:12-16,19-21). If we do not grow in love, we show that we do not know God. God's love brought us life, and His love in us guarantees that we will love one another.

Our need for God's love is actually critical because we are not talking about the "nice warm feeling" kind of love that the world means when it misuses the word. God's love is strong, challenging, and true. God's love in our life is what breaks our self-centeredness and pride, and though these forces are not completely eradicated in this life, God promises that as we abide in His Word we are set free from their domination. Only through transformation in God's love are we able to control the self-centeredness and pride, so we begin to place others' needs before our own. *That* is what love is all about.

In my first pastorate I had a rude awakening as I tried to counsel Christian people to love in this way. One couple I counseled had been married over fifty years, and as I explored their difficulties it came down to one primary issue: The husband said, "I just don't love her anymore." He had loved her for many years, but now he had "run out" of love.

In many ways, I understood their plight because of my own marriage. Lynne and I met when I was only a two-week-old Christian. We were married ten months later. The pastor who married us gave us only one hour of premarital counseling. And so we had to learn even the simplest principles of married life the hard way.

I was such a brand-new Christian that few areas of my life were trained by the Spirit of God. One area that needed radical change was my temper. I had a bad temper from the time I was a little boy. In my first months as a new Christian I was so immersed in my new life that Lynne never saw the temper. But when we got married my immaturity began to show itself. During that first year of marriage, I would get so frustrated and angry that I'd look for the first thing available to take my rage out on. (After every major argument, the trash man knew about it because he found pieces of broken furniture at the curb.)

During that year I lived in fear that Lynne would leave me. My family history is full of people who left. My mother had two husbands walk out on her, one of whom was my own father who walked out six months before I was born and never came back. My older brother walked out on his wife, and my younger brother's first wife walked out on him. I was afraid that Lynne would finally get fed up with my stupidity and leave.

But it was then that I began to understand God's love for the first time. Lynne had God's heart, a heart that never stopped loving. God's love continued to pour into her heart, which she then was able to pour out to me, in patience, kindness, soft answers, and spiritual guidance. She wasn't foolish, and wouldn't place herself in a position where she could be hurt—but her love was the example I needed of how love worked. It changed me forever. I was a jerk. I didn't deserve her love. Yet she committed herself to me and helped me to become the person God wanted me to be. For twenty years, the fruit of her yieldedness to God has been a husband whose heart and life have been transformed by love!

That is God's love: a love that will not walk away, a love that is committed to people, a love that will not rest until it produces God's character in those who are loved.

Do You Want to Grow in Love?

Change the Kind of Love You Practice. Love, from God's perspective, is primarily an action. Paul tells us that "God has poured out his love into our hearts by the Holy Spirit whom he has given us. . . . God demonstrates his own love for us in this: While we were still sinners, Christ died for us" (Romans 5:5,8). God's *actions* are the evidence of love.

As Jesus' followers, then, we can define love this way:

> Love is an unconditional commitment to an imperfect person; a commitment I give myself to in order to bring the relationship to God's intended purpose.

On many occasions I have assured couples that they could put their marriage back together in a healthy manner if they would commit and give themselves unconditionally to God and to each other.

I urge you to consider carefully Jesus' commitment to us. While we were yet sinners He died for us. In dying for us He showed His love, and His love has made a change in our hearts so that we now can love with His love.

Allow Love to Change Your Heart. We must acknowledge what the apostle John declares: we love, not because we are such naturally loving people, but because God first loved us (1 John 4:19).

Our heart is changed in the first place by letting God's love enter our lives. We are awed and profoundly humbled as we meditate on the truth that God entered history to die a brutal death in our place. How can we not love and trust and surrender all to a God who loves like this—with such vulnerability, so giving of Himself? And how can we refuse to give such love to others? As the new spirit God has placed in us feeds on these awesome truths, our heart becomes like God's heart. This transformation of love is the work of God that occurs deep within us. Do you see how our heart then grows as we intentionally orient our lives toward God?

To know and experience the love of God is to open our heart to the treasure of His love. Jesus declared that what we value is our treasure, and our heart will continually be attached to what we value: "where your treasure is, there your heart will be also" (Matthew 6:19-21).

We fill our hearts with God's treasure by understanding how much He values us and the people in our lives—so much that He gave Himself for us. Fill your thoughts with God's values and set goals for daily life that adopt God's values.

I saw real change in my relationship with Lynne when I began to change my values. We had been married for about two-and-a-half years. Our first child had been born and my wife was home with our baby, but she also took in typing and odd jobs to help financially. I was in my first year of seminary and I worked full-time to help make ends meet. It was a very busy time of our lives and quite stressful. It would have been easy to let the demands of life crowd out our relationship. But we began to set one hour aside every evening just to talk and connect with each other. It didn't matter if we had other pressing commitments. If we had been irritated with each other we tried to talk it out. If one of us was at the breaking point of stress we tried to help each other deal with the issues. That sacred hour gave us the opportunity to express our commitment, our love, to each other.

That one hour a day was worth far more than sixty minutes. The hour set aside by both of us showed what we valued and gave us a regular time each day to demonstrate what our love for each other meant. It showed that we valued each other, a healthy relationship, and open communication. (It gave me the opportunity to express myself in ways more productive than throwing a temper tantrum!) We continue this practice to this day, and it is tangible evidence of the fact that we have reoriented our hearts in order to share God's love with each other. I value our relationship, and I want Lynne to know it. I will never stop loving her as I act from a heart that has been transformed and is continually filled with God's love.

God is love. And He is infinite. So He has an infinite supply of love. As we open our heart to Him, His love pours into our heart and overflows to those around us.

Fruit: Transformation of Character

The third result of our new life in Jesus is "fruit," that is, actions that are consistent with the nature and will of God. As we abide in Jesus' Spirit we experience a transformation of character by which we're empowered to bear fruit (John 15:7-8).

During that fateful final night with His disciples, Jesus promised that those who remain attached to Him would continually experience His life flowing through them. He used the metaphor of the vine and branches, where He is the life-giving vine and His disciples are the fruit-bearing branches:

> "I am the vine; you are the branches. If a man remains in me and I in him, he will bear much fruit; apart from me you can do nothing. . . . This is to my Father's glory, that you bear much fruit, showing yourselves to be my disciples."
> (John 15:5,8)

Fruit bearing is the outward and visible sign of a believer-disciple. What kind of fruit will we produce in keeping with Jesus' life in us?

Fruit of the Spirit. The *fruit of the Spirit* are those characteristics produced by the Spirit of God which enable us to be more like Jesus in our daily lives. "The fruit of the Spirit is love, joy, peace, patience, kindness, goodness, faithfulness, gentleness and self-control" (Galatians 5:22-23). The singular form—"fruit" not "fruits"—stresses that these qualities are a unity, like a bunch of grapes instead of separate pieces of fruit. As a whole they will be found in all Christians.

I may have some of these characteristics because of my personality makeup, but the profound truth is that you and I will experience the transformation of our entire character as we allow the Spirit to operate in us. When we help people to understand the workings of the Spirit and show them how to be filled with the Spirit, the fruit of the Spirit will be produced naturally in the individual disciple as well as in the life of the church.

Fruit of Righteousness and Good Works. Paul prayed that the Philippians would be "filled with the fruit of righteousness that comes through Jesus Christ" (Philippians 1:11) and that the Colossians' lives would be "bearing fruit in every good work" (Colossians 1:10). Jesus' life in us will produce His own righteousness in our lives and will enable us to live in such a way that our daily lives are full of good works.

What is "righteousness"? Jesus issued a challenge in the Sermon on the Mount: "Unless your *righteousness* surpasses that of the Pharisees and the teachers of the law, you will certainly not enter the kingdom of heaven" (Matthew 5:20). These men understood that the person who knew God's standards for life and then lived up to them was righteous. Who could be more righteous than the Pharisees, with all their good works?

But Jesus was looking beyond man's works to the perfect work God would accomplish at Calvary—He looked ahead to the righteousness a person can have only through faith in Jesus' blood. Our own righteousness and good works can accomplish nothing of eternal value, but when His righteousness is imputed to our account, we are declared righteous in God's eyes.

As the righteousness and life of Jesus become increasingly central in our priorities, the Spirit of God will cause us to become like Him in our personal righteousness and in our service toward others. We are made new creatures in Christ by His grace and are now enabled to grow in our personal righteousness and do good works for the kingdom of God (Ephesians 2:8-10).

Fruit of a New Generation of Disciples. The *fruit of a new generation of disciples* will be produced by God through us as Jesus' life transforms our objectives in life. When Jesus looked on the masses of people all around Him who had not yet responded to His invitation to follow Him, He demonstrated a heart of compassion (Matthew 9:35-38). Yes, Jesus knew that this crowd of people were sinners, and He also knew that the crowds would soon call for His own crucifixion (Matthew 27:20-26). Yet Jesus knew their need of salvation and spiritual healing even more than they knew it themselves. So He went to where those people lived, and He gave them a message of hope and transformation.

That's the kind of heart we can have. Sometimes we look at nonChristians around us as the enemy. We need to see nonChristians through Jesus' eyes. We are no different than they are, except for the work of God's grace in our lives. As we allow Jesus' heart for the lost to characterize our heart, we will be compelled to be involved in our world, carrying the message and ministry of Jesus to the lost, so God can produce the fruit of conversion through us.

As Jesus opened the Samaritan woman's spiritual eyes to see that He was the Messiah, offering her eternal life, she and many other Samaritans from her village became believers. But Jesus' disciples were aghast that He, a Jewish man, entered into conversation with a Samaritan woman. They were so overwhelmed by their own personal prejudices that they could not understand she was a woman in need of spiritual life. Jesus rebuked them by saying:

> "I tell you, open your eyes and look at the fields! They are ripe for harvest. Even now the reaper draws his wages, even now he harvests the crop for eternal life, so that the sower and the reaper may be glad together." (John 4:35-36)

Jesus has called us not simply for our own eternal reward but also to engage with Him in planting the seed of the gospel and to engage ourselves actively in watering, nurturing, and harvesting the next generation of disciples. True, we each have different roles, but we are all vessels of hope for the world.

Do You Want to Grow Fruit?

Using the brilliant analogy of a vine and its branches, Jesus allows us to see that when we have new life, we *will* bear fruit as a natural result. Dead branches don't bear fruit. The fruit suggests a guaranteed natural product of the Spirit, made possible by the living relationship between the Christian and God. A tree doesn't have to hope for fruit, it will bear fruit naturally. A Christian is now a new creature, born of the Spirit, and so he or she will bear Spirit-fruit, not flesh-fruit (Galatians 5:16-26).

But as a vine needs proper nutrients, water, light, trimming, and positioning, so does the Christian. A vine is dependent on others to help it grow. While there will be many times that other believers will come to us to help us grow, in large part we are responsible for getting in the place where we can receive the proper nutrients (Word of God), water (ministry of the Spirit), light (fellowship with Jesus), trimming (confession of sin; effort to do away with the habits of the old man), and positioning (fellowship with believers; out of the path of sinners).

When we take care to place ourselves in right conjunction with God's resources we will change and grow and the fruit will come naturally. This also means we have a responsibility to nurture and care for others by providing the right environment for fruit to be produced in their lives.

What strategy could you implement to allow the Holy Spirit more freedom in developing the fruit of biblical discipleship? Consider the following:

Nurturing the Fruit of the Spirit. Consider Galatians 5:16-26, comparing carefully the works of the flesh (especially verses 19-21) and the fruit of the Spirit (verses 22-23). Develop a personal consciousness about the works of the flesh in your life. Try developing one aspect of the fruit of the Spirit each week for the next nine weeks. Study the biblical meaning of each and then focus upon that one aspect for the week, seeking ways to practice it. Pray specifically for the Holy Spirit to show you how to demonstrate it in your life.

For instance, consider a person who irritates you or with whom you are angry. Ask God to help you see the cause of irritation or anger in you. Maybe it is your own perfectionism or your lack of care for the person. Ask other Christians to help you talk through the issues. Wisely determine what action should be taken, what attitudes need to be adjusted, and what needs to be left to the Spirit alone to change. You will find that you will grow in attitude and actions with such a practice.

Nurturing the Fruit of Righteousness and Good Works. What evidence of righteousness and good works is apparent in your personal life? What evidence of these is found in your home life? How can they be nurtured? Try thinking of God's standard for each of your personal actions during an ordinary day. When I go into a meeting that I know has people in it who are somewhat hostile to me, I have to prepare myself to be in control of my thoughts toward those people and the words that I speak. I have to consciously ask the Spirit to give me a right attitude, to control my tongue, and to give me a clear understanding of the issues so that I am not sidetracked by personal agendas. Overall I am asking, What is God's standard for my participation in the meeting? I have confidence that the Spirit will be there throughout the meeting, helping me to accomplish my best.

We are speaking here of Christlike character. We are responsible for our willingness, but the Spirit enables us to go beyond even our natural abilities (Philippians 1:11; Colossians 1:10).

Nurturing the Next Generation. Are you more comfortable with Christians or nonChristians? Is that a good or bad sign? How are you and your family reaching out to nonChristians with Jesus' good news? Talk about how you can keep free from the evil of the world, while at the same time impact the world around you with Jesus' good news.

Realistic Transformation

The biblical truths we have discussed in this chapter are what make it possible for you and me to become like Jesus. I have centered my personal life and ministry life on these truths and have found them to be liberating and realistic.

The beginning of transformation is Spirit-produced new life as we are born again to the kingdom of God. The evidences of transformation in our lives are threefold. The first evidence is *freedom*, which results from a transformation of our mind and will. The truth of the Word of God sets us free from the lies of the world and enables us to direct our lives toward God and His ways. The second evidence is *love*, which results from Jesus' love transforming our heart. He gives us an endless supply of His love. The third evidence is *fruit*, which results from the Spirit transforming our character, producing personal righteousness and good works, and a new generation of disciples. I believe that these truths are at the center of the Christian life.

I am convinced that many people do not believe that this kind of life is realistic. There are at least two reasons for this.

In the *first* place, many people have not experienced this kind of personal transformation themselves. Among the reasons why the earliest disciples deserted Jesus at the cross was that they did not know what was available to them in order to live truly as Jesus' disciples. With the coming of the full ministry of the Holy Spirit at Pentecost, they knew what was available and were forever changed.

Even with the emphasis upon the spectacular ministry of the Spirit in recent years, I do not see an emphasis upon personal transformation. We need a clear understanding of what the Spirit is doing, from the initiation of our new life to the nurturing of our transformation.

In the *second* place, we are ignorant of the practical ministry of the Spirit. We need to get the kinks out of our lives which hinder the normal operation of the Spirit. Let me use a simple illustration to show you what I mean.

When we place our limbs in an unnatural position we put kinks in our arteries and vessels; these kinks hinder the normal flow of blood. The hindered flow of blood weakens the muscle temporarily, even rendering it useless for a short time. When we put our limbs back into a natural position we take the kinks out so the blood can circulate naturally, and strength and usefulness return.

When our limbs are in a natural position, we don't sense the blood's flow at all. The only times we notice it are when we put kinks in the flow or when we exert ourselves beyond normal operation.

This is a picture of the Spirit's operation. Every Christian has the Spirit (Romans 8:9-11). In the normal operation of the Spirit we will not always sense His work. When we are called to a special activity we will sometimes sense His presence more consciously.

When we sin we place ourselves in an unnatural position and quench the Spirit's flow in our lives. He does not leave us, but He cannot help us function in the normal way because we have blocked His operation. We are not living as we should, whether through conscious sin or ignoring our relationship with God.

But the Spirit won't leave us alone. He will convict us of our sin and even discipline us to get us to wake up and confess our sin. When we straighten out our lives the Spirit rushes to help us live as we should, but it may take us some time to get back to normal. His operation in our lives helps us to live in freedom and love while we bear fruit.

Individual transformation through the Spirit is a realistic expectation of the New Testament. Now let's get the kinks out! Join me in this miraculous transformation of our lives!

A Beginning Exercise In Freedom

As a beginning exercise in comparing the words of the world with the Word of God, try resolving some of the issues below.

Marriage. What makes up a truly Christian marriage? What are the values that would characterize such a marriage? Should a Christian ever date a nonChristian? Marry a nonChristian? What is your love for your spouse like? Is it possible to "fall out of love" with your spouse? Is it ever appropriate for a Christian to get a divorce? Remarry?

Family. How important is your family to you? If you were to establish realistic priorities for your life, where would your family rank? What ranking do you believe the Bible gives for your family? How can you, on a daily basis, give biblical priority to your family? What should be the role of the Christian family in light of the recent trends in public and governmental influences? How should the church, and you, respond to the gay movement? What would you do if your daughter announced she was a lesbian?

Material possessions. What is the most important material possession that you own? Why? What does the Bible say about wealth? Is it bad or good? How should you use material possessions? What kind of car should a Christian drive? Why? In what kind of house and neighborhood should a Christian live? Should you save so that you can leave an inheritance for your children, or should you give your inheritance to Christian ministries?

Social activities. Do your neighbors and fellow workers know that you are a Christian? How do they know? What is appropriate social behavior for a Christian? Is it appropriate for your children to engage in sporting activities on Sunday? Is it appropriate for Christians to drink socially? Where and when?

Continued on next page

Continued from previous page

Self-image. How do you feel about yourself? Do you like yourself? Why or why not? How does God feel about you? What are the ways in which the world tries to develop a positive self-image? What should we do to develop a positive self-image? What is appropriate to do to take care of problems we might have (overweight, bad skin, personality quirks, cleft palate, large nose, etc.)? When do we tell our children simply to ignore influences from culture and "be themselves"?

Care for the poor. How do you feel when a person on the street comes up to you and asks for money for something to eat? What do you normally do? What is your attitude toward the homeless? Who should care for the poor in your neighborhood?

Education. How important is education in your development as a Christian? What role does education play in preparing us for life? For ministry? Should you send your children to public or private schools? What about homeschooling? Should Christians attend secular universities? Should public schools teach both evolution and creation? What should private Christian schools teach?

Abortion and euthanasia. What is the beginning point of human life? When does life end? How should we show the value of life as Christians? Is abortion ever to be advocated? Why? When? Should you attempt to keep your 85-year-old father who has had a massive stroke and whose brain waves are almost nonexistent on life support?

CHAPTER EIGHT

THE PROCESS OF BECOMING HUMAN

...in the beginning when He willed, God made [man] who was not; and much more readily will He restore again him who had existed, when He wills that life be given him.

IRENAEUS,
AGAINST HERESIES (CIRCA A.D. 190)[1]

■

Earlier in this book, I suggested a definition of discipleship that went like this:

> Discipleship means living a fully human life in this world in union with Jesus Christ and His people, growing in conformity to His image, and helping others to know and become like Jesus.

The first time I gave that definition in public, while teaching a doctoral seminar in the Philippines for international students, one student—an exuberant teacher from a Bible college in Irian Jaya—had difficulty with one part of the definition.

"Professor Wilkins," he said, "I am troubled by the phrase, 'living a fully human life.' My students are converts from paganism. I don't want them to live more *humanly*. I want them to live more *spiritually*."

Over the years, the one part of this definition that consistently is questioned is the expression, "living a fully human life." I can easily understand the concerns that Christians have about the expression. Since many of us are so aware of our sinfulness in this life, we tend to equate the sinful nature with our humanness. But this is a misguided understanding of our humanness. A better understanding comes from the intriguing statement of the early church father Irenaeus in the second century:

> "The glory of God is a human being fully alive."

When I first heard that statement quoted in a sermon, I puzzled over it for some time. But then I read Irenaeus' statement in the light of a profound declaration from the apostle Paul, that man is "the image and glory of God" (1 Corinthians 11:7).

Paul looks back on the creation accounts and concludes that humans, created in the image of God, are the glory of God in this world. The very *purpose of our existence* is to manifest the glory of God in this world. We are His workmanship, God's creation, and so we bring praise and honor to God by living life fully as our Creator intended us to live it. New Testament scholar Gordon Fee insists, "By creating man in his own image God set his own glory in man. Man, therefore, exists to God's praise and honor, and is to live in relationship to God so as to be his glory."[2]

This is similar to the way in which a work of art is an artist's glory, since it both gives expression to a part of the artist, and at the same time brings praise and honor to the artist's skills simply by being what it was intended to be.[3]

Read this statement carefully, thoughtfully: Our *humanness* should not be considered inherently sinful. We have a *sinful nature* as a result of the Fall. However, the original creation of man and woman in the image of God did not include sin as a part of their nature. At their creation God declared them to be "very good" (Genesis 1:31).

One urgency I feel, which has led me to write this book, is a desire to help us all understand more clearly the kind of discipleship Jesus initiated, a process of growth that actually helps us to become more human. First, we are more connected to God, spirit to Spirit. And this makes us more healthy, whole, and free as persons, more effective in the daily roles of life (father, mother, husband, wife, employer, employee) and more in tune with the rest of God's creation.

Sadly, many of our Christian teachings and activities actually encourage the opposite. They are so removed from regular activities of life that they create a false dichotomy between *human* life and *Christian* life. Remember the stale old cliché, "He's so heavenly minded he's no earthly good"? Biblical discipleship has as its goal to make us heavenly minded *and* earthly good.

I recognize in Irenaeus' statement at least two profound truths which guide my life and spiritual growth.

First, humans are created in the image of God with a central purpose for our existence, which is to manifest the glory of God in this world. Connected to Him, we are to become more fully alive, and the more fully alive we are, the more others see the glory of God in us. So we must understand what it means to be fully human as *created* in the image of God.

Second, as the perfect God-man, Jesus is the example for us in His humanity of what it means to be fully alive to *display* the glory of God. Therefore, we will also explore how we can fully develop our humanity so that we can become more like Jesus.

In the Image of God

The revolutionary truth that we can become like Jesus takes us into the depths of God's purposes for humanity. When God said, "Let us make man in our image, after our likeness" (Genesis 1:26), He was designating a special purpose for, and relationship with, humans in His creation.

> So God created man in his own image,
> in the image of God he created him;
> male and female he created them.
> God blessed them and said to them, "Be fruitful and increase in number; fill the earth and subdue it. Rule over the fish of the sea and the birds of the air and over every living creature that moves on the ground." (Genesis 1:27-28)

Humans are like God and represent God in a way unlike any other creature. The image of God is something in our very nature as humans, in the way that man and woman were originally created.[4] It refers to what we *are*, rather than something we *have* or *do*.

How *are* we like God in ways that make us different from the rest of creation? Think of the differences between you and your favorite pet. Lately my wife's cat, Maui, has taken a special liking to me and my study. While I am working at home she comes into my study with me.

When I go to make a sandwich for lunch she follows me, expecting to have lunch with me. When I go back to the study she follows me in for her afternoon nap. Someone observing external behavior might think that Maui and I were quite alike.

Although we have similarities as creatures of God, there are specific ways in which Maui the cat and I are *quite* different. These differences hint at aspects of my existence which are created in the image of God.[5]

Mental aspects. Augustine argues that the human rational faculty distinguishes humanity the most from the animal kingdom. He suggests that the central distinctive element of human nature is our God-given ability to relate to God. We have the ability to reason, think, and learn in ways unique to us. We use abstract, complex language; we are aware of the distant future; and we have creativity in areas such as art, music, literature, and science which distinguishes us from animals. We also have an emotional makeup that, to a very large degree, makes us more like God than like any animals.

Moral aspects. We humans are morally accountable before God for our actions, and we have an inner sense of right and wrong which is unique to us. We are like God when we act according to God's moral standards because our behavior is holy and righteous before Him. But our unlikeness to God is reflected whenever we sin.

Spiritual aspects. Humans have an immaterial spirit in addition to our physical body which allows us to operate in the spiritual realm of existence. It is our spiritual life which enables us to relate to God on a personal level. The person who has not yet entered into that spiritual realm of existence has not yet engaged his or her full humanness. This is vital: We are fully human only when we operate in the spiritual world as well as in the material world.

Relational aspects. Not only are we unique when we engage in a spiritual relationship with God, but we have the possibility of healthy relationships with other humans. The intimacy of marriage, the functioning of a believing family, the community of the believers worshiping God together all point to a complexity and depth that mirrors the relationship of the Godhead and the relationship of God to His people. This is different from our relationship to the rest of creation, which we are called to rule as God's caretakers.

Physical aspects. Many theologians also argue that the human physical body is also included as a part of what it means to be made in the image of God. Since our body is a part of our whole person, it contains aspects of the way we are like God. While God has no body because He is Spirit (John 4:24; Exodus 20:4), our body reflects something of God's character. Our body is necessary to rule over and care for the rest of creation. Our body enables us to be like God who, although He is without a body, sees, speaks, hears, and moves. We are more like God in these ways than any of the rest of creation.

You and I, as human beings created in the image of God, are the glory of God in this world. We have been crowned with glory and honor (Psalm 8:5), and when we are most fully alive to God, He is given honor. Why then do we not see most humans glorifying God?

The Image of God Is Distorted

When we, as God's special creatures, sinned, it had a profound effect upon the image of God. Sin distorted the image of God in humans by affecting every aspect of our likeness to Him. The biblical concept of sin is rebellion against a holy God, transgression against God's laws, a basic bias against righteousness. Our moral purity has been lost, our intellect has been distorted with falsehood and pride, our relationships have been tainted with selfishness. Indeed, we can say that the essence of sin is self-centeredness and pride. And so we are less like God now than before sin entered the world.

On the other hand, however, men and women did not *lose* the image of God because of their sin. After the worldwide flood, God established a death penalty for murder among human beings which was based on the fact that humans retained the image of God. God said, "Whoever sheds the blood of man, by man shall his blood be shed; for in the image of God has God made man" (Genesis 9:6). James condemns the way humans hurt each other with our tongue because when we curse each other we are offending humans who are "made in God's likeness" (James 3:9).

You and I today are humans created in the image of God. Yet while we still retain the likeness to God, it has been profoundly distorted because sin affects every aspect of it.

Restoring the Image of God

How amazing, then, when we turn to the New Testament and see that a restoration process has begun with our redemption in Christ. As we have seen, we received new life in Christ, which is the beginning of the transformation that we experience in this life. Paul tells us that as Christians we have received a new nature that is "being renewed in knowledge in the image of its Creator" (Colossians 3:10).

As we grow in understanding God, His Word, and His world, we begin to think more and more of the thoughts that God Himself thinks, and so we are being "renewed in knowledge." This is a description of the normal Christian life, not something out of the ordinary. Throughout this life God intends that we continue to grow in likeness to Christ, "being transformed into his likeness with ever-increasing glory" (2 Corinthians 3:18).

This process is referred to theologically as *sanctification.* But it is not simply a theological curiosity. The Puritan theological giant John Owen indicates how the restoration process now makes a practical difference in our daily lives:

> Sanctification is an immediate work of the Spirit of God on the souls of believers, purifying and cleansing their natures from the pollution and uncleanness of sin, renewing in them the image of God, and thereby enabling them from a spiritual and habitual principle of Grace, to yield obedience unto God.[6]

We are set free to be alive to God through a process that reverses the distortion and restores the image of God in us.

Ultimately the image of God will be completely restored in our eternal, glorified state because we will be "conformed to the likeness of his Son" (Romans 8:29). The apostle John looks ahead to the coming of our Lord Jesus at the end of the age and says that we will then be transformed to be like Him:

> Dear friends, now we are children of God, and what we will be has not yet been made known. But we know that when he appears, we shall be like him, for we shall see him as he is. Everyone who has this hope in him purifies himself, just as he is pure. (1 John 3:2-3)

This has been God's goal for you and me from the beginning. Since we already are created in the image of God, our new birth is the process of restoring the image of God in us to what it should have been, and even taking us beyond as the process of perfecting us to be like Christ is completed (1 Corinthians 15:49).[7]

Restoration—And a Full Human Life

There are several implications that arise from understanding who we are as humans, created and restored in the image of God.[8]

The purpose for which we were created is ultimately to be in relationship with God. Therefore, we experience *less* than our full humanity when we are apart from God. In that sense Christians are capable of becoming the most fully human persons on earth because a central aspect of our existence is being restored to us.

Men and women are most fully human when they enter into a relationship with Jesus Christ. Male and female—from every race and culture on earth—are made in the image of God. This is what makes for true equality of persons. And it is why we insist that all humans have an inherent value to God. All human life is sacred. God declared that murder was punishable by death because it concerned taking the life of a person made in the image of God (Genesis 9:6).

That we are of value to God should not produce arrogance in us, but rather it should motivate us to help others be restored to their full potential. Our concern for our fellow humans is in part driven by our concern for their wholeness since the New Testament makes it clear that God will restore the damaged image in all those who turn to Him for healing (2 Corinthians 3:18). The heart of the human does not have peace until it finds its rest in the One to whom we belong. Jesus said, "Render to Caesar the things that are Caesar's, and to God the things that are God's." Jesus was saying in effect, "Give your money to Caesar since it has his image on it. It belongs to him. But give yourselves to God because you bear His image and you belong to Him."

There Is a Dignity in Being Human

We belong to God and we bear His image in the depths of our humanness; realizing this fact should give us a profound sense of dignity, worth, and significance. We are important to God and we are supremely important in the outworking of His universal program of history. Evolutionists would make us only animals which originated by chance. Geneticists reduce us to programmed chemical compounds. But when we reflect rightly on the fact that we are created in the image of God, we should stand amazed that God made something like Him, and that we are more like Him than all the rest of creation. At the same time, this should cause us to treat our fellow humans with the same dignity, worth, and significance that God has extended to us. Kindness, courtesy, and respect are proper ways of treating persons who have the innate dignity of being created in the image of God. John Bunyan spoke wisely, "Dost thou see a soul that has the image of God in him? Love him, love him; say, 'This man and I must go to heaven one day.'"[9]

One of C. S. Lewis' most profound sermons was "The Weight of Glory," given in Oxford during the war in 1941. Lewis calls for us to consider the glory of human beings created in the image of God. Such a consideration should cause us not only to contemplate our own potential glory hereafter but also to think about our neighbor in the here and now. Lewis says:

> The load, or weight, or burden of my neighbor's glory should be laid daily on my back, a load so heavy that only humility can carry it, and the backs of the proud will be broken. . . . Next to the Blessed Sacrament itself, your neighbor is the holiest object presented to your senses. If he is your Christian neighbor he is holy in almost the same way, for in him also Christ—the glorifier and the glorified, Glory Himself, is truly hidden.[10]

You are a person with special significance to God. People may ignore you or overlook how special you really are. Your insight to a discussion might be treated flippantly. It might seem like no one really knows you exist. But God does. Start with finding your sense of worth and dignity in God's eyes and in His purposes for your life. That will allow you to start to live with confidence. In turn, it will help you to give to others around you the respect and dignity they deserve as your fellow creatures. David felt that he had little personal significance in the grand scheme of the universe, until he recognized his value to the God who created him in His image and wanted to use him as His chosen instrument in this world (Psalm 8:3-8).

Sometimes, as Christians we may tend to look down upon people who are not yet believers, limiting our contact because they are not saved. That is wrong.

The brilliant French mathematician Blaise Pascal, following his own dramatic conversion to Christ (1654), argued that the heart of every human is incomplete and miserable until it finds its rest in God. The unbeliever may not be consciously aware of it, but that is the way we are when we are apart from God. This has become a classic assertion, and I believe that it is especially important to observe when we interact with nonChristians. Deep in their heart, in the way that God has created them, unbelievers have an inherent sensitivity to spiritual things, and they cannot find their rest until they find their completeness through the work of the Spirit in their heart. Unfortunately many are seduced by spiritual counterfeits.

All of this should make us even more eager to reach out to those around us to help them find their rest in God through the true Spirit of God. Regardless of how hardened a person may *appear* to be toward God and spiritual things, the Spirit still convicts people of sin, righteousness, and judgment (John 16:7-11). Because of our creation in the image of God, any person who has not responded to the Spirit yearns for a spiritual aspect of life. We are fully human only when we relate to God through His Spirit.

Patterning Ourselves After Jesus

To become a fully human and fully alive person, then, we pattern ourselves after Jesus. He is the complete revelation of the image of God (Colossians 1:15-20), and at the same time He is the one person whose humanity was never spoiled by sinning (Hebrews 4:15). Since the outworking of the image of God is seen most fully in Jesus, we should pattern ourselves after Him. In addition to the points we raised earlier in chapter four, consider some more ways Jesus sets a perfect example for us:

- Jesus had perfect fellowship with the Father. (John 17)
- Jesus obeyed the Father's will perfectly. (Luke 22:42; John 4:34; 5:30; 6:38)
- Jesus had unswayable determination to fulfill the work which the Father had sent Him to accomplish. (John 9:4)
- Jesus always displayed a strong love for humans, regardless of whether they were lost, sick, sorrowing, or sinful. (Matthew 9:36; 10:6; Mark 1:41; Luke 7:13)
- Jesus' love was demonstrated by freely giving up His life for us. (John 15:13)

This is the image of God in its purest sense, and as we imitate Jesus in these attitudes it will form His likeness in us (Romans 8:29).[11] Jesus experienced human development as we do, yet perfectly, so we have the perfect example in Him of what it means to be fully human.

As foreign as the words may seem to many of us at first, *discipleship* does mean living a fully human life in this world in union with Jesus Christ. Discipleship is not meant to make us more religious and dutiful. It is the path to real life. The disciple of Jesus Christ can be the most fully alive of all humans. Professor Millard Erickson observes,

> Every human being is God's creature made in God's own image. God endowed each of us with the powers of personality that make possible worship and service of our Creator. When we are using those powers to those ends, we are most fully what God intended us to be. It is then that we are most completely human.[12]

Back to Our Full Development

We are talking about how to be more effective in every area of life, not just so-called "spiritual" areas. So let's look at three specific ways that discipleship to Jesus can allow us to develop as fully human persons, fulfilling God's destiny for us.

First, we can develop as *whole persons*. We saw in chapter three that Jesus' early years are an example of the way in which all of us should develop as whole persons. Luke 2:52 tells us that Jesus grew in . . .

- Wisdom = Intellectually
- Stature = Physically
- Favor with God = Spiritually
- Favor with men = Socially/Emotionally

The majority of discipleship programs, at most, focus on only one or two of these areas.

For example, the literature of certain ministries discusses discipleship as a one-on-one relationship in which a more mature Christian "disciples" another Christian. This one-on-one relationship can take many forms: weekly Bible study together, prayer, accountability in the disciplines, discussing a significant book, or mentoring a younger colleague in ministry skills. These types of one-on-one relationships are important, but they tend to involve mostly the mental or intellectual dimension of a person's life.

Other church and parachurch ministries emphasize small groups as the most effective means of discipleship. Many of the same activities found in a one-on-one relationship occur here as well, with an emphasis on intellectual activities. Small groups have the advantage of promoting more personal interaction with a wider spectrum of persons. This heightens the relational or social features of a person.

While these activities each contribute to the personal growth in specific areas, we can be more intentional about developing in *every* area of life.

Several years ago I accidentally stumbled across a relationship that helped me develop the most as a whole person. I had just taken my first full-time teaching position. I was stretched to the maximum of my ability to prepare for all new courses, to make ends meet financially, and to try to be a good father and husband. I was growing rapidly intellectually and spiritually but suffering in other areas. I wasn't getting any exercise, I didn't have time for my friends, and I didn't take any time out to enjoy myself.

My wife was getting concerned, so she and one of my closest friends, Ken, got together and conspired how to help me out. They made me commit to spending three hours with Ken every Saturday morning. When Ken arrived at 6:00 A.M. I had cups of coffee for us. We drove to one of our favorite surf spots where we finished our coffee and caught up on the week. Just before we paddled out to surf we stood and prayed together. We surfed for an hour or two. Not only did I get exercise, but we laughed and hooted and hollered for each other as we rode the waves.

While waiting for the next set of waves we talked about our personal lives and professional lives. Ken was single when we started, but eventually he got engaged and married. I helped him think through the transitions of his life, and he helped me to keep a right perspective on my marriage and family. Ken was a businessman, I was a professor. As different as our professional worlds were, we helped each other to think through our responsibilities and purpose in life under God. Ken was a lay leader working with a singles group in his church, while I was an ordained minister. But in each other's eyes, and before God, we were equals in every way.

Because our commitment was to help each other become healthier *in all aspects of life*, some of the best spiritual counsel and support I received came from Ken during those talks while waiting for the next wave. He pushed me to pray for my students and to be interested in their personal lives, instead of simply playing out a professorial role with them. When my father was dying Ken gave me a view of God's compassion that enabled me to be a support to a man whom I had never known.

Those Saturday mornings with Ken lasted for about seven years. Eventually the patterns of our lives wouldn't let us keep it up. I look back on those years with the fondest of memories and also with a clearer understanding of what it means to be a human being fully alive. My wife always said that I was a much different person when I got back. She wasn't jealous for my time away because it helped me to be a better person. And I learned lessons that remain with me today about how to develop as a whole man.

I encourage you to think through your patterns of life. What are your strengths? What areas of your life need to be strengthened? Perhaps you are naturally more of a people person. You probably become vulnerable to people because of your natural care for them. Who do you turn to to receive comfort when you have been hurt? Who pumps you back up spiritually and emotionally after you have become depleted? Your individual characteristics, personality traits, and even occupational orientation require balancing. You need "whole person" nurturing. Consider what steps need to be taken to round out your life so that you can develop as a whole person.

The kind of discipleship I am talking about is not at all about a particular program. Discipleship may include programs, but discipleship is the development of *real life* over a period of time. Programs can help in some ways as we attempt to apply principles of discipleship. But discipleship, as an integrative process, synthesizes a variety of programs and methods over a period of time to develop well-rounded persons. You and I were made to function in an integrated manner. Each of our human attributes naturally influences the others.

Does your life include developing relational, or emotional, or intellectual elements? As you understand the needs, hurts, struggles, and longings of the people for whom you pray, you will find yourself making the commitment to involve yourself in their lives as God directs you. We cannot develop our spiritual life without it affecting every other area of our lives. Many of our programs do not help us to be fully integrated persons because they try to develop the spiritual life separately from the rest of our makeup.

Make Intentional Transitions through All Stages of Life

Discipleship is a process to be developed intentionally over one's entire life span. It helps us transition through, and maximize, all the stages and responsibilities of life in order to arrive at the goal of becoming like Jesus.

As I have interacted with a variety of organizations over the years, one of the heartbreaks that they share with me is that they see large dropout rates among their members. Discipleship programs and ministries are quite helpful for one particular stage but often do not prepare people for the next stage(s), and so people drop out.

This is especially true for discipleship ministries that work with college students. Many ministries have become highly successful over the years at evangelizing and equipping college students. These students experience a high degree of accountability, activity, and fellowship. However, once they graduate and go out into the ranks of society, many drop out of Christian activities.

A number of reasons are given for the dropout phenomenon. These students often have not been involved in a local church, so they don't easily assimilate into a local fellowship. Also, when they get into society they are not regularly around other intensely committed Christians, so they do not receive the support necessary to live in an everyday setting. College campus ministries focus on the particular stage of life associated with the college student. (The major questions are: Who am I? What will I do with my life? Why am I here?) However, they tend not to prepare the disciple for moving on into everyday life where other issues are more pressing (that is, finances, job market, a dysfunctional employer).

Discipleship involves the entire life span of a person, helping her or him transition through all stages of life and all the responsibilities of life. A church or parachurch ministry could do no greater good for their people than preparing them to be well-rounded disciples of Jesus in all the circumstances of life.

- Do we help high school students prepare for the challenges of their college years? Do we help college students transition to the routines of societal life?

- Do we hold young people accountable to receive extensive premarital counseling before we perform their wedding?
- Do we actively prepare young couples for the overwhelming responsibilities of parenting in today's world?
- Do we offer help for parents who face an empty nest, grandparenting, and retirement?

I asked some of these questions to a mixed adult group recently, and I was overwhelmed by the response. With all of the Bible studies, fellowship groups, prayer chains, and committees that met regularly in the church, most of the people in the group said that they were not given any help in preparing for the next stage of their lives.

One older lady in particular caught my attention. She said that no one warned her how difficult it would be to function without a car. Her family decided that she was too old to drive. They put her in a retirement home several miles away from her neighborhood, friends, and church. Since there is only limited public transportation where she lives, she can't get to the store, she can't get to church, and she can't even go to visit her friends. She had been one of the most vibrant and active older ladies in the church, but now she feels worthless as a human being. She cannot be a participant in even the simplest activities of life.

She needs to understand that God has a purpose for her regardless of the stage of life she faces, and we need to be much more intentional about preparing people for their next stages of life. The process of becoming like Jesus does not stop in this life until the day we go to be with Him.

The ultimate goal of our spiritual formation is not to master any one program or curriculum. Rather, it is to continue opening ourselves to God, in the character of Jesus, as we experience all areas and all seasons of life. The kind of life Jesus has come to offer us is this: A life that leads us to the fullness of our potential as humans created in the image of God.

Consider carefully how this applies to you. Have you given attention to the growth of your overall personal life—intellectually, physically, spiritually, socially, and emotionally? Are you fully alive to God, His people, His creation, and His calling for you? It doesn't matter whether you are a homemaker or a construction worker. A salesman or a sailor. A student or a waitress. A pastor or even a prisoner.

As Irenaeus said, "*The glory of God is a human being fully alive.*"

CHAPTER NINE

FULLY TRAINED IN COMMUNITIES OF FAITH

You might already have discovered for yourself how radically different traveling alone is from traveling together. I have found over and over again how hard it is to be truly faithful to Jesus when I am alone. I need my brothers or sisters to pray with me, to speak with me about the spiritual task at hand, and to challenge me to stay pure in mind, heart, and body.

HENRI NOUWEN,
IN THE NAME OF JESUS (A.D. 1989)[1]

■

"Mike, is there any way you could stop by here on your way back home from the East Coast?" The voice on the other end of the phone call belonged to my older brother, Bill. Curiously, he seemed unusually subdued.

"Sure I can make the stop. Why, what's up?" I asked.

He paused for a moment. "I just got back from the doctor. It doesn't look good." Another long pause. Then Bill almost whispered, "This is going to be a tough one. I have AIDS."

I grew up with two brothers. I was in the middle, with two years separating me from both my younger brother, Tim, and my older brother, Bill. At various times growing up, the three of us rotated as best friends. At other times we fought like crazy. I think we were pretty typical brothers. All in all, I look back on our times together and realize that we had a wonderful thing going.

One of the factors that kept us close was that we needed each other. We didn't realize it then, but we had a pretty difficult home life. My biological father was an alcoholic and, as I mentioned earlier, he left us before I was born. My first stepfather physically abused my mom and us boys. He left on Christmas Eve when I was in seventh grade.

My mom is a tender, but tough, woman. She spent much of her

childhood in Children's Hospital in Los Angeles. She lay in bed for months at a time in a body cast from head to foot because she had contracted tuberculosis of the bone. She taught us to be tough, to take whatever challenges life threw our way, and she taught us how to stand on our own.

She also taught us to take care of each other. No matter how unruly and wild we three boys became (and we were pretty wild), she was always there to stand by us when we needed her. When I think of my mom, the word that comes to mind is "loyal." She was loyal and taught us to be loyal to each other.

So my brother Bill's phone call was a natural part of the way we had been raised.

But there is much more to the story. You see, fifteen years earlier Bill and I had a falling out. He and I became Christians at about the same time. It was during the turbulent time of the late 1960s and early 1970s. We were immersed in our new life as Jesus freaks.

But then something snapped. Bill went away for a weekend to spend time with old friends from high school. When he came back, Bill announced to us in the family that he was leaving. I'll never forget his words. "I've been thinking about other people all my life. It's time that I started thinking about myself." (He was only twenty-five!) Bill had decided that he was going to leave everything to find his own happiness.

I blew up. I got in his face and called him a weak, self-centered fool. We always pretty much said what we felt, and I let him have it. But that time Bill didn't fight back. He just took it.

Only later did I realize that something far deeper was going on. The next day he took his wife aside to tell her that he had warred for years with feelings of homosexuality. In my own immaturity I had no idea of the struggle that had worn him down from within.

Bill left: He left his wife, turned away from our family, left his schooling, gave up on his promising career as an architect, turned his back on the Lord, and went off to pursue independence and pleasure. He traveled all over the world to pursue activities and philosophies and pleasures. So we became estranged. I couldn't accept what he had done to others. I was still a young Christian then, and I overreacted. I had told Bill, in essence, "If you don't need us, we don't need you." Because I felt he'd rejected us, in my stubbornness I turned away from him.

Contact was limited and very cool. At our grandmother's funeral,

Bill said to me, "Mike, there's a wall between us. You don't accept me."

I had thought about this many times over the years. I responded, "Bill, I love you as deeply, perhaps even *more* deeply today than ever before. I accept you and love you as my brother. There is absolutely no wall between us as *brothers*. On the other hand, I don't accept your lifestyle. I feel responsible to protect my family from your disease and from your philosophy. And so I do put up a wall . . . to protect *them*."

Bill took a long look at me and said, simply, "Oh. Is that all? I understand that. I can accept that. I can't force my ways on you. But I just needed to know that you still love me as your brother."

This left us with a difficult situation. Over the years I believed that I had taken a right stand on the issues. At the same time, I had become so consumed with my stand that I confused Bill *as a person* with the issues concerning his *lifestyle*.

Other Christians may not understand or agree with me, but from that point on I learned that there were certain points in our relationship where Bill and I could be reconciled. We could love each other in many ways in spite of our differences. I still believe that Bill bought into a philosophical and religious lie that destroyed his life, but we were reconciled as brothers.

Over the next year-and-a-half I flew to visit Bill several times. He had moved to be near our mom and brother Tim, who took wonderful care of him. I spent the final weekend with Bill in an AIDS hospice house. What a horrible disease to see in the final stages. Just before he slipped into a coma, Bill asked me to lean down next to him. He whispered, "Mike, thanks for being here. Thanks for loving me."

He died the next day.

Individualism and Community

The reconciliation with Bill was both a signal and a symptom of a big step in my spiritual growth in Christ; which is to say, it was a huge growth step toward being a whole human being who is filled by the Spirit.

People in families grow closer to each other and develop into the individuals they were meant to be when they learn to rely on each other, to help, challenge, and be loyal to each other.

People need each other. I hadn't always believed that. I used to think that I didn't need anyone, and no one should need me. My personal theme when I was a kid was captured by Simon and Garfunkel's lyric, "I am a rock, I am an island." That was my youthful arrogance, maybe born out of hurt. I preferred to walk alone, to need no one, and to have no one need me.

But going through the challenge of my brother's illness and death over a period of years showed me I needed my family and they needed me. David Gill stated the principle wisely: "The challenges we face are formidable; without community they become impossible."[2]

People need each other to share the good times and to support each other through the hard times.

When I came back from that weekend when Bill died, I needed the comfort and strength and fellowship of *both* my families—my biological family and my spiritual family. My wife and children, and mother and brother understand me better than anyone else. They could cry with me and laugh with me as we recalled memories of Bill at family gatherings. I shared their grief, and they shared mine.

But I also needed my expanded spiritual family, I needed the comfort and strength and fellowship of my brothers and sisters in Christ. One of my closest friends where I teach recently lost his daughter to a tragic death. We found a strength and comfort in each other that we desperately needed because we understood each other's grief and sorrow. We helped each other with the difficult questions of "why," and we talked through our personal reactions to our own emotions. We didn't have to go through the grief alone. Walking with Jesus in the realities of life requires both an individual relationship with Him as well as a community relationship with other disciples. I used to think, "Jesus and me! That's all I need." But over the years I have come to realize God never intended that kind of solitary individualism. From the very beginning of His ministry Jesus called men and women into a relationship which was intended to be developed both with Him personally and also within a family of other disciples.

Our growth in Christ is intended to be developed within these two families: the spiritual family and the biological family.

A Spiritual Family—and Our Natural Family

Jesus took the Old Testament family covenant theme established through Abraham's blood line (Genesis 12:1-3; 17:1-16) and broadened it to initiate a new sort of family community. On one occasion while Jesus was talking to the crowd, He pointed to His disciples and said, "Here are my mother and my brothers. For whoever does the will of my Father in heaven is my brother and sister and mother" (Matthew 12:49-50).

Within the group of disciples we can see concentric circles around Jesus. In the outer circle are the large number of disciples who believed in Jesus and became His followers. Then we find seventy-two who were sent out on a preaching tour (Luke 10:1-17) and a group of women who traveled with Jesus and the Twelve to support their missionary tour (Luke 8:1-3). Then we find the Twelve trained as apostles (Luke 6:13). These concentric circles did not indicate levels of spirituality; all disciples were equal but some had specialized ministries.

We also find an inner circle gathered around Jesus, made up of Peter, James, John, and sometimes Andrew. This inner circle seems to have had an additional role, which is seen clearly at one of the most intense times of Jesus' earthly life. Just prior to His betrayal, arrest, and crucifixion, Jesus took the disciples with Him to the Garden of Gethsemane. He took Peter, James, and John further into the garden with Him to pray. He said to them, "Sit here and keep watch with me" (Matthew 26:38). Jesus brought the inner group to share this difficult time with Him, wanting their fellowship, support, and encouragement as they watched with Him. Sadly, they failed Him. New Testament scholar Leon Morris states:

> There is a sense in which [Jesus] had to be alone in prayer, for only he could pray the prayer he prayed. But there is also a sense in which he could have been encouraged by the support of his closest followers nearby.[3]

This may be hard for us to understand, but Jesus needed them. Although He had to carry His own load, He needed the support and fellowship of His closest companions.

Jesus broke down barriers—economic, racial, religious, gender—by calling people into a spiritual family based on equality. There are different ministry roles within the family, but each person, as a disciple, has equal value as a family member. The spiritual family of disciples today is called the church. We are brothers and sisters in Christ; we need each other as a spiritual community of faith (see Hebrews 10:24-25).

As Jesus formed a family of faith based on the new birth, He continued to uphold the biological family. From Old Testament to New Testament, the earthly family plays a major role in God's program for humanity. The family played a foundational role in raising succeeding generations to know the will of God and the importance of community life.

Although Jesus was to have top priority in individuals' lives (Luke 14:26), He did not intend to sever all earthly family relationships. Pairs of brothers were called to be among the Twelve (Matthew 4:18-22), Peter maintained a family relationship with his wife and mother-in-law (Mark 1:29-31), and Jesus directed the apostle John to care for His own earthly mother, Mary, after His death (John 19:26-27). When Jesus rebuked the Pharisees who were not caring properly for their parents, He validated the command of the decalogue: "Honor your father and your mother" (Matthew 15:3-9; Ephesians 6:2).

The biological family was designed to nurture God's children to know the will of God. It was also designed as the primary influence upon children to help them grow as whole persons. Secular social scientists recognize this influence. In the words of one expert, family is

> the most profound of all influences on who we are and what we do. . . . The families to which we are born and those in which we live as adults shape us from birth to death. They are the immediate cause of our best and worst times.[4]

Since the family is one of the most influential forces on our lives, a most natural place to develop disciples of Jesus is in the home. In the same way that spiritual family members help each other, biological family members need each other in the process of growing in Christ.

Let's see how this can be done.

Discipleship at Home

The discipleship process begins in the home as husbands and wives help each other to grow in their likeness to Christ (Ephesians 5:21-33). We don't often think of discipleship as a part of marriage, but who has better opportunity on a day-to-day basis to influence every aspect of your life than your spouse?

My wife and I started developing a relationship two weeks after I became a Christian. We were both in our early twenties. She had been a Christian since she was a little girl, but I was a brand-new baby in Christ. She helped me to learn the Bible and to overcome bad habits from my old life (like swearing) so that my attitude and actions were more Christlike. I helped her to overcome a deadness in her spiritual life as she experienced a fresh approach to Jesus and to her Christian lifestyle. Our mutual discipling relationship was vital as we adjusted to marriage, children, and careers.

If you are married, have you considered your marriage to be a mutual discipling relationship? You are influencing each other already. Why not make it intentionally *supportive, positive,* and aimed at growth into *whole, healthy personhood*? In the context of urging his readers to follow Christ's example, the apostle Peter speaks to married readers and encourages them to influence each other to be more Christlike in their individual lives and in their marriages (1 Peter 2:21–3:7). We can learn from Peter's advice.

Peter tells wives: If you have a husband who is now disobedient to the Lord, you will influence him far more effectively by your behavior than by all of the words you might speak. Your nagging him about going to church might drive him away. What changes in your daily attitude toward him might be more Christlike? Your inner purity of thought and values are your true beauty (1 Peter 3:1-6).

Peter likewise gives advice to husbands: If you do not respect your wife and give her opportunity to grow, you are not really walking with God yourself; as a result your prayers will be hindered (1 Peter 3:7).

No one in the last twenty-five years has had more opportunity on a daily basis to impact me than my wife. But we have to be intentional about helping each other, and we have to be open to the influence from each other. Let me suggest several ways to get started.

First, set aside one evening a week as "work on marriage night." Find an evening (or make one!) that you will get together every week for two to three hours. Make it your primary intention to grow in your relationship. (This is a good practice for engaged couples to start and to take into marriage.) Put this evening on both of your calendars and don't allow anything else to usurp it. Commitment to this priority is vital.

Second, for your first few weeks read a good book on marriage, such as Larry Crabb's *The Marriage Builder*, or Jack and Carole Mayhall's

Marriage Takes More than Love, or Norman Wright's *Communication: Key to Your Marriage*. Agree on the chapter to be read during the week, and then during your "work on marriage night" talk about the issues raised and how they can be put into your marriage.

Third, husbands, I suggest that you take a lead in bringing this about. Not in a domineering way, but simply by making sure that it happens. Husbands need to find positive, active ways to exercise spiritual leadership in the home. And don't bring a militaristic, corporate executive attitude—take the more relaxed attitude of simple care and support. Your motive should always be *love*, not forcing your wife to grow. Your attitude will make or break this time of exchange where personal growth can take place.

Fourth, pray for each other. As you finish up your time, share personal needs you would like your spouse to pray for. Pray together out loud. Keep track of those prayers weekly and see how God answers them.

Fifth, look for ways during the week to encourage each other in the issues that were raised during your evening together. *This does not mean nagging or criticizing!* Part of your own growth is to find positive ways to encourage and support each other.

Sixth, vary the format as the weeks and months and years go by. One evening you might go out to dinner to talk. Another time you might go for a walk at your favorite park or lake or beach. You might also vary the agenda by going to a marriage workshop for a weekend or for several weeks during your scheduled evening.

There are many specific ways that you and your spouse can help each other to grow in Christ. The important thing is to be *intentional* about doing it; then be *consistent* and *creative* in finding ways to carry it out.

The Parent as Discipler

As husbands and wives help each other, they are preparing themselves to disciple their children in healthy spiritual growth (Ephesians 6:1-4). Parents lead their children toward Jesus, introduce them to Him, and prepare them for life with Him after they leave home. Let me say it plainly: We lead best by personal example and that means living lives that are changing and growing in godliness and love. Then our words are not clanging with emptiness (1 Corinthians 13), but they ring with the authority of *authenticity*.

The primary responsibility for discipling children does *not* belong to the church; it belongs to parents. No one has more opportunity on a day-by-day basis to form the life of a child than parents. Since this includes every aspect of a child's life, parents have the opportunity to help that child grow to become like Jesus in every area of life: intellectually, emotionally, physically, and spiritually. The church simply cannot do what parents can do naturally. Take your children to Sunday school and vacation Bible school. Get them involved in youth groups at church. These activities will provide invaluable influences on your child's life. But these activities last at most for only a few hours a week. You have them most of the time from the moment they are born. You have an opportunity to influence them in every area of life so that they grow to be godly, balanced men and women.

Parenting is the opportunity for the most whole-life application of discipleship possible. For Lynne and me, parenting definitely includes regular times of prayer and discussion of biblical truths. But it also includes helping our daughters think through issues for a research paper on the Nazi holocaust or on national welfare. It involves working together to drywall our garage and repair the plumbing. It includes exposing them to the wonders of God's creation on a camping trip to the mountains or a drive through the desert. Parenting encompasses teaching our daughters how to ride a bike or snow ski, as much as it involves guidance on who to date or how much makeup to use. Discussion of our family finances with our daughters naturally includes biblical principles concerning money, envy, priorities, goals in life, and the value of temporal and eternal life. We avoid using clichés and support them rather than manipulate them with guilt-inducing techniques. But underneath every discussion lies our biblical foundation.

I encourage you to be *intentional* about the attitudes and values and examples you are living out before your children. The seriousness of our desire to raise our children to be spiritually alive and growing people will be reflected in our determination to help them know and cooperate with God's will in every area of their lives.

How important is the role of parent-as-discipler? How far-reaching is our potential influence?

The apostle Paul repeatedly emphasized the need for the leaders of the church to have their family relationships in order. In the lists of qualifications for leaders in the church we find a specific emphasis upon the provenness of elders and deacons in the home. Marriages are to be solid, and children and households are to be in order (1 Timothy 3:4-5,12; Titus 1:6-7).

Paul is not simply laying down arbitrary qualifications. The training ground for leadership in the church is leadership at home. The healthiest, strongest leaders in the church will be those individuals who grew in Christ by learning the process of discipleship in the home. Those of us who have not been raised in Christian homes will be able to learn firsthand from leaders in the church who have healthy spiritual, emotional, and physical lives. They are the ones who can pass on those principles to us (2 Timothy 1:5; 2:2).

The Church's Role in Discipling Families

We need to clarify the relationship between discipleship in the home and discipleship in the church (or in parachurch groups). Both of God's institutions—the biological family and the spiritual family—have been ordained for the role of providing guidance in growth. We are healthiest and strongest when we learn to balance both.

Jesus said that a disciple, when fully equipped, will be like the master (Luke 6:40). The expression "fully equipped" speaks to the various aspects in which we grow as individuals who are emerging into godliness. The expression is strikingly similar to the corporate process of discipleship found in the church. Gifted persons (especially pastor-teachers) have been given to the church for the full equipping of the saints in the work of service, to the building up of the body of Christ (Ephesians 4:11-13).[5]

- A disciple when "fully equipped" will be like the master, Jesus.

  ↙ ↘

  Individual process of discipleship

- Jesus gave gifted persons for the "full equipping" of the saints for ministry.

  ↙ ↘

  Corporate process of discipleship

When we apply this to the relationship between the church and the family, we see that the responsibility of the church is to equip families so that husbands and wives can disciple each other and so that parents can disciple their own children (Ephesians 5:21–6:4).

The equipping of families involves training them to know the full teaching of Scripture so that they can in turn live out this truth in their everyday worlds. Churches and parachurch ministries will need to develop strategies by which the biblical truth about every area of life is made accessible to families. (In chapter seven we discussed some practical ways that we can learn the truth and live the truth.) Individual disciples and families cannot obey the truth unless they know the truth.

Once we know the truth, disciples need to be trained on how to obey the truth and how to practice the truth in relationship to other persons in the body. Sunday school, youth groups, and summer camps all provide invaluable specialized training for children in areas of life that parents are not able to provide. Charles Sell's book, *Family Ministry*,[6] offers practical ways of providing just such a ministry to families. These ministries are invaluable, but the realities of daily life require guidance from parents who are on the scene day to day. We will discuss momentarily some of these avenues of discipleship, like creativity, modeling, mentoring, and empathy.

I want to emphasize that it is also the obligation of the spiritual family to offer help when the biological family cannot fulfill all of its responsibilities. I immediately think of single-parent families within our churches. Widows and widowers have experienced enough tragedy with the loss of their spouses, but they often do not receive much support beyond the funeral service as they attempt to raise their children alone. And while we might deplore the breakdown of marriages both within and outside the church, the reality is that we have an explosion of single-parent families from divorce all around us. The ministry of many churches and parachurch ministries when it comes to these single-parent families is mostly nonexistent. As I have looked back on messages I have given in churches and conferences over the years, I realize that I did not regularly include principles that helped single parents. I didn't really include them into my mental picture, so their needs were left out. The answer, in part, may be specialized classes within our churches or specialized conferences at retreat centers to give focused help to their particular needs. But we must also enfold these single-parent families within the regular fellowship of the body.

All in all, our job is to be supportive of all families, including families that are not able to fulfill all of their responsibilities. We can also include here the burgeoning senior citizen population, older widows and widowers, and the young person who does not have Christian parents. Each of these require special equipping because the biological family may not be able to carry the load.

Discipleship in Community

Essentially, growing in Christ does not, cannot, take place in a vacuum. Loving God must spill into loving people, or it is not the real love of God at all (1 John 4:7-21). That's why we must insist that the most important principles of discipleship be taught in the context of both the biological and the spiritual family.[7]

We could list innumerable principles of community discipleship, but I suggest these eight:

- Creativity
- Mentoring
- Modeling
- Empathy
- Accountability
- Mutuality
- Trust
- Letting go

We will discuss the first four in this chapter and the last four in the next chapter in the light of our responsibility to live out our discipleship to Jesus in God's world.

Creativity

Creativity is an essential ingredient in helping others grow in Christ. Because of the tremendous diversity of callings and services God has in mind for His people, we must be creative as He uses us to spread His invisible kingdom over the earth, to every walk of life. Since each member of the body is unique and different from the others, each should be treated with the uniqueness due him or her (1 Corinthians 12:12-27). How much creativity is needed as you disciple your children? Each child has unique individual characteristics, parents have their own backgrounds and personalities, and our society and culture exert a powerful additional influence. At any particular time these dynamic forces vary, so we must be creative when helping our children grow according to their own individuality.

We can help our children find their place in society and give them an inner grounding that will not allow them to compromise the biblical values associated with the family.

General principles of community life can be applied to both the spiritual and biological family. Commitment to group goals and purposes larger than ourselves is part of healthy growth. Yet we must keep in mind that God has purposes for each person, and we must remain committed to training and guiding each person in our discipleship communities as an individual.

What general principles of healthy growth can be applied to your child? You might think of many that apply to all children, such as loving nurture, appropriate discipline, instilled responsibility, and a balance of physical discipline, emotional security, and intellectual stimulation. At the same time, what are the ways in which your child is unique? Perhaps she is very shy. What will it take to draw her out and help her be more confident? Or perhaps your son is strong willed. How can you help him develop self-control and consideration for other people? Maybe your spouse experienced a severe emotional trauma in his or her early years. What can you do to encourage healing from the traumatic memories, while helping overcome fear, anger, grief, depression, or an inability to adjust to adult life? Each person needs special attention in his or her individualized growth. As we grow through the various stages of life, we will meet different needs and challenges. That is why our spiritual guidance needs to be open and creative, not canned and programmatic.

Mentoring

Mentoring is one of the most familiar forms of a discipling relationship, and it occurs in a variety of contexts. It is often a one-on-one relationship by which a more mature, experienced person guides the development of another person in a particular area of life. For example, we have a program on our faculty where more experienced professors develop a mentoring relationship with younger faculty, helping them to develop into mature professors. The mentoring includes training in specific skills necessary for the profession, but it also includes attention given to the development of personal character.

Mentoring is an essential element of the spiritual community. As older pastors work with younger staff, they pass on to them proficiency in skills of ministry but also include forming the personal life of the younger person. Consider Paul's classic statement to the young pastor, Timothy:

> You then, my son, be strong in the grace that is in Christ Jesus. And the things you have heard me say in the presence of many witnesses entrust to reliable men who will also be qualified to teach others. (2 Timothy 2:1-2)

Paul's relationship to Timothy is often cited as a central discipleship model for the church. It is an aspect of discipleship, since it involves disciples. But more accurately, this is leadership/discipleship development through mentoring. Paul is directing Timothy as a pastor to recall how he had been trained for ministry and in turn to prepare others for service to Christ.

Mentoring is also a crucial part of marriage and parenting. It is only in the last fifty years—with increased urbanization, technology, and higher education—that boys and girls have had people other than parents to mentor them in *household skills* and *family trades*. This is not inherently a bad thing because it does expose children to a wider range of skills. However, it certainly has contributed to the weakening of family relationships.

Recently a young high school girl in our neighborhood told us that her career of choice is to become a homemaker. Part of what's driving her in this direction is a negative experience in her own family life. She remembers having only baby-sitters with her at home during the day from the time she was a baby all the way to the present. Her mother and father both had to work. She says that when she gets married and has children she wants to be home with her children when they grow up so she can have more influence in their lives. She respects her mother greatly and wishes she could have had more contact with her when she was growing up.

Mentoring in the home also includes *character development*. In this way we provide our children an example, showing how we have gone through the process of human development ourselves and become well-balanced, mature Christian adults. This includes helping them understand how we have overcome weaknesses, as well as how we have developed our strengths. While much of this is intuitive, we can be more effective when we take the time to reflect upon our development, trying to ascertain what has been most helpful and what has been detrimental. This takes a great deal of personal analysis, but it allows us to provide intentional guidance by reflecting upon our own personal process.

This is why a mother or father often says, "Well, when I was a girl/boy . . . ," and then goes on to relate an incident from her or his own childhood. This is also true of other forms of mentoring, such as when a preacher uses his own life as an example in a sermon, or when a counselor in a counseling context relates her own experience, or when a corporate executive draws upon his business experience when nurturing younger staff persons. We are trying to use our own experience as an example, and it helps us to enter into the other person's world.

We must be careful to remember, though, that as much as our experiences are similar to other people's, their experience and calling will always be unique. We must also be careful not to force our children or other adults into a mold that is formed by our experiences. Creativity allows us to help shape a person's life in line with his or her individuality.

Modeling

Closely related to mentoring is the need for *modeling*. When the apostle Paul wrote to the church at Corinth, "Be imitators of me, just as I also am of Christ" (1 Corinthians 11:1), he was using his life and actions as an example for the church to follow when faced with difficult lifestyle decisions.

Try to imagine yourself going into your local church this next week, standing up in front of the congregation, and saying, "I would like all of you to imitate my life from now on." Some might accuse you of being presumptuous and arrogant! Why? Since you are not perfect, you are not worthy of absolute imitation.

Was Paul being presumptuous and arrogant? No. Because, in the first place, he told them to imitate him only *insofar* as he imitated Christ. They were always, primarily, to imitate Jesus. Second, Paul is not overstepping his place because imitating each other is a regular part of our everyday lives. We all need examples in life, and when we pattern ourselves after others, we have learned from the example they have set for us.

Obviously this can be taken too far. I know of a large church with a rather despotic pastor. It is almost humorous to see young men in his church all but literally preach like the pastor, spout his same doctrinal party lines, and attack anyone who deviates from the pastor's policies and practices. I say almost humorous because I have watched sadly as many of these young men go into their own churches and create havoc.

Properly presented, giving others a human example of how to grow in Christ is invaluable. I thrill to watch my daughters treat others with almost the same kindness that my wife regularly offers to people around her. Both of our daughters, when they were young, approached us on separate occasions to ask us to help them invite Jesus into their heart. They said, almost identically, that since they knew we had Jesus in our hearts, they wanted Jesus in theirs.

Of course, we must be aware of *all* the implications of modeling because our example can also be negative. I cringe when I see my daughters not control their tempers in the middle of a difficult situation in the same way that they have seen me react in the past. It gives me an opportunity to help them learn, as I have. But I must accept the fact that unknowingly they have imitated me in small negative ways every day of my life with them.

Nonetheless, modeling can be a potent force in giving each other an example of healthy living and Christian character in the everyday details of life. Life is the workshop in which we show each other how the Christian life works.

Try communicating to your spouse, *silently*, for an entire week, "The way I treat you this week is the way that I would like for you to treat me." For an entire day each time you are with your children *silently* say to them in each activity, "I would like for you to imitate my attitude and my actions. The way that I deal with people and life is the way that I would like for you to deal with people and life. I would like for you to have the same relationship with God that I have."

Whether you actually say so or not, each day you live in front of your children or spouse or friends at church you are saying, "Imitate me." Each time you stand before a class to teach, each day you live in front of your neighbors, each working day at the office, you are saying, "Imitate me." For what we are really saying loudly with our lives is, "Imitate me as I imitate Christ."

Empathy

Another essential practice to learn in our community of disciples is empathy. Empathy involves entering into another's experience to feel with them about their situation.

I learned two of the most important words in my marriage during our third year together. It was a difficult time. I was going to school full-time and working full-time. Our first child was only a year old. Lynne had quit her job to be home with our newborn daughter, but she also worked part-time from our home. We had long, long hours with very little relaxation or free time.

One day I came in from classes before going to work. Lynne had tears in her eyes, she was holding a crying baby, we had very little food, and it was an extremely hot, uncomfortable day in our little rental house.

She blurted out, "I'm tired of all of this! We never get a break, we're always working, we never can even take a day off! I'm going home to my mom to get away from all of this for a while!"

Now, you have to understand what I am like. I am a very controlled person. I don't show much emotion. At the same time, I like to have an answer for all problems. And when Lynne has a problem like the one she was displaying, I like to sit her down and give a list of ten ways to overcome her reaction. (This does not usually work well.)

However, that day, as I looked at her and her situation, I only said two words: "I understand."

Lynne's reaction was classic. She almost completely stopped crying and asked, "What did you say?"

"I understand," I repeated.

We then sat down, and I listened to what she'd gone through that day. After she talked, I asked, "Do you want me to call your mom to see when it's all right for you to go home?"

"Go home?" she asked. "I'm not going home. This is my home. I just needed you to *understand*."

Empathy means to place ourselves on common ground with others—whether in the church or with our own family—and say, "I understand." It means to enter into their world and give ourselves to them. Paul said to his beloved church at Thessalonica, "We loved you so much that we were delighted to share with you, not only the gospel of God but our lives as well, because you had become so dear to us" (1 Thessalonians 2:8).

When we enter into another person's world we do not leave our own. We just share theirs. When we enter into our child's world, it is not to become a child. We remain an adult, which allows us to have a mature perspective from which we can provide insight and help. But we become one with them in their world of circumstances. They know we understand.

Implications

These four principles are our beginning point for practicing community discipleship: *creativity, mentoring, modeling*, and *empathy*. We will discuss four others, *accountability, mutuality, trust*, and *letting go*, in the next chapter.

Before we focus on the implications of these relationship and growth principles, I am reminded of one of the trips I made to visit my brother Bill before he died.

I hadn't seen Bill for about four months, and as the door to his apartment opened, I saw standing before me a skinny old man, bent over, shuffling along with a cane, almost bald. It was Bill. If he had walked toward me on the street I never would have recognized him. Bill had been 6'2", he had weighed about 180 pounds, he had been an outstanding athlete, great looking, in marvelous shape. He had even been a model for a men's clothing magazine for a while. But now the disease had ravaged him. He would eventually look like a refugee from a Nazi concentration camp.

All that day we talked about his condition, about old memories, about everything. We laughed . . . and we also cried. At one point Bill talked of the mistakes, the lost potential. He said, "I know that I have been gifted with so much, and yet, I have wasted my life because of the mistaken choices I've made."

How tragic, I thought, that he made life choices without really knowing the consequences. How much different would it have been if people who loved him could have helped him work through the issues?

At one point Bill said, "Mike, I'm sorry that I had to put the family through all of my misery."

At Bill's funeral, our other brother Tim shared with us a video he had made of Bill's life. He had pieced together old photographs from our earliest childhood up till just before Bill died. Those forty-one years of Bill's life seemed but a fleeting shadow. The video showed both the good and the bad times, and our laughter and tears mingled as we watched. Tim had selected one of our old favorite songs to play in the background while the video unfolded the pictures of Bill's life. The primary line to the song was, "He ain't heavy, he's my brother."

That line should be a theme song for us, for all people, in the family of faith.

I have been changed by the experience with my brother. I hope that as I have shared it you have seen that I now have a deeper understanding of discipleship as it is lived in relationship with others of God's family. The implications of our involvement in communities of faith are crucial for our personal and corporate spiritual growth. Let me conclude by summarizing those implications:

- *First*, we will find the greatest fulfillment in our relationships only when we recognize that Christ must be at the center. How will you practice the presence of Jesus in your family relationships?
- *Second*, God has called you as a unique person to meet the needs of your family, whether it is the biological or spiritual family. How can you use your God-given uniqueness to meet the needs of your spouse and children, brothers, sisters, and parents? How can you use your uniqueness to serve the people of your church? God is in the business of forming unique communities of faith.
- *Third*, we need each other. In what ways do you need your spouse? In what ways does your spouse need you? Learn how to meet each other's needs without having to ask them. How can you give yourself to meet the needs of your children as they go through the difficult times of life?

Remember, the challenges we face in life are formidable: Without community they become impossible. We need each other in the process of becoming like Jesus.

CHAPTER TEN

INTENTIONAL SOJOURNING IN GOD'S WORLD

There is a combination of virtues strangely mixed in every lively holy Christian, and that is diligence in worldly business and yet deadness to the world; such a mystery as none can read but they that know it.

JOHN COTTON,
CHRISTIAN CALLING (CIRCA A.D. 1650)[1]

■

Superbowl Sunday is almost a national holiday here in the United States! Friends and neighbors gather together for the big game. Some avidly watch the game. Others come only because they like a party. In fact, many who come don't know much of anything about football.

At one Superbowl party a little girl suddenly spoke up. "Why are all those big men standing in a circle holding hands?" Seen from her perspective, it did look funny when huge, six foot, six inch, three-hundred-pound linemen stood holding hands in the huddle!

To the uninitiated the huddle in football may seem to have an insignificant role. For all one knows, they might simply be taking a quick break. But the huddle actually plays an invaluable role.

In the huddle the players straighten out miscommunication and figure out how to stop a blitzing linebacker. The huddle gives them a chance to regroup and give a second effort. Those big linemen hold each other's hands to indicate that they are united. They are a team; they support and hold each other up. The huddle is also where they get the play for the next offensive effort. All the players get their assignments so they can move the ball down the field.

As invaluable as the huddle is to the football game, it is only effective when they break out of the huddle, get into formation, and carry out the play. Even if the team knows it will get pounded on the next play, they can't stay in the safety of the huddle. They have to go play the game!

Going out is the final nonnegotiable of biblical discipleship: Our life of growth in Christ is carried out in God's world.

On occasion I've heard the church referred to somewhat sarcastically as a "holy huddle." The speaker or writer is belittling Christians who hide away from the world in the safety of their own little gatherings. I, too, am sometimes distressed to see Christians hiding away. But in this chapter I want to use the huddle in a positive way. Our "holy huddle" will perform an invaluable service for us when we use it for support *and* preparation. Discipleship is not something for the cloister; rather, it is something to be lived out in the world. *Disciples are intentional sojourners in God's world.* It is one thing to declare yourself to be a Christian within the church or among other Christian friends. It is another thing to live that commitment out in the world. This can be accomplished by proper training, a proper concern for the world, and proper guidance while living in this world.

Purposeful Gathering

Like the football team, we need to gather together regularly. We need the fellowship. We need to recuperate from the temptations and chaotic circumstances of living in a fallen world. We need the encouragement that we receive from other believers who love us and support us. Hebrews gives a striking perspective of our gathering together.

> Let us hold unswervingly to the hope we profess, for he who promised is faithful. And let us consider how we may spur one another on toward love and good deeds. Let us not give up meeting together, as some are in the habit of doing, but let us encourage one another—and all the more as you see the Day approaching. (Hebrews 10:23-25)

We stand shoulder to shoulder with other believers, often holding hands, often giving each other a hug and a holy kiss from the Lord. In our gathering we support each other through our difficult times, our times of defeat or struggle. It is also when we celebrate life's victories.

Week by week we meet to worship and receive the preparation necessary for our lives. Pastor-teachers carefully examine the Word of God and give us truth by which we can live. When I was a pastor, I focused on one primary principle of life that I could impart to my people in the sermon that would encourage them and give them direction for the coming week. That principle would then be applied throughout the week in various ways by the diverse people of the congregation. Yet we were all going in the same direction because of the wonderful, living Word of God.

Nonetheless, our purpose in life is not to *stay* gathered away in our meetings. Rather, it is to become stronger in order to advance, to be salt and light, to live before a watching world in the way God intended life to be lived.

Consider what Jesus prayed for His disciples on the night before His crucifixion:

> "My prayer is not that you take them out of the world but that you protect them from the evil one. They are not of the world, even as I am not of it. Sanctify them by the truth; your word is truth. As you sent me into the world, I have sent them into the world. . . . My prayer is not for them alone. I pray also for those who will believe in me through their message, that all of them may be one, Father, just as you are in me and I am in you. May they also be in us *so that the world may believe* that you have sent me." (John 17:15-21, emphasis added)

Jesus' prayer is the basis for the expression that has marked Christians through the centuries: We are to be *in the world* but not *of the world.*

Our gathering together has a number of purposes, not least of which is fellowship, encouragement, and receiving instructions for life. But we have to get out there in the world if we are going make an impact.

A friend of mine runs a ministry adjacent to the University of Virginia. Students from the university come to be with other believers to be equipped from the Word of God. They want to know the truth so that they are able to evaluate from God's perspectives their education and culture. My friend's purpose is not to keep them away from the university. His overriding purpose is to get them well-established in the faith so that they can go back to the campus, and eventually go into society, as strong young Christian men and women.

Over the years, I have noticed that many discipleship programs have tended to pull disciples *out* of the world by creating a mini-world within church or parachurch activities. True, we all need to be in the secure company of other believers. And yet we must resist the tendency to gather believers away in order to build up the ministry, making them ministry-dependent, instead of equipping them to live life in the world.

As ministries become more effective at helping individuals and families to walk with Jesus in the world, the church reaches out to the world instead of withdrawing to itself.

Combining the emphasis upon community we discussed in the last chapter with the emphasis upon reaching the world in this chapter, we might act on these principles in a way that looks like this:

- Church community equips ——► family communities ——► to disciple their own families ——► to make a new generation of disciples in this world.

- Church community equips ——► workers ——► to reach the world.

How is this carried out?

Intentional Sojourners

A mission of Jesus' disciples is to go make more disciples of all the nations. In this earthly life each of us is but a sojourner, says the psalmist—literally, a resident alien (Psalm 39:12).

Now the creation awaits its renewal and it groans under bondage to sin and decay (Romans 8:19-22). We, however, live as people who have been set free from death and sin. Our transformation has already begun. Therefore, we really are at this time *not of this world.* Paul says that "our citizenship is in heaven" (Philippians 3:20), and Peter calls us "aliens and strangers in the world" (1 Peter 2:11). The future will be different when our Lord Jesus returns, but for now we live as sojourners in a hostile world. The following practices help us to live effectively as sojourners.

A sojourner attitude must not cause us to escape from the world by withdrawing to ourselves. Remember the huddle analogy. We come together to receive training so that we can live with an outward perspective, not a desire to turn inward to escape. Peter goes on to say,

> Dear friends, I urge you, as aliens and strangers in the world, to abstain from sinful desires, which war against your soul. Live such good lives among the pagans that, though they accuse you of doing wrong, they may see your good deeds and glorify God on the day he visits us. (1 Peter 2:11-12)

Our growth and transformation in Christ is what enables us to live effectively as God's children in this world. When you develop your identity in Christ you will not go seeking it in the world. When you experience liberation from the lies of the world through the truth of the Word of God and the transforming power of the Spirit, you will not be entrapped by the temptations of the world. You will be able to go where people live and work and play to reach them with the gospel. Our transformation enables us to prepare ourselves to live in the world, and "live such good lives among the pagans that . . . they may see your good deeds and glorify God."

A sojourner loves the world, but not the world system. In the apostle John's first letter he says:

> Do not love the world, nor the things in the world. If any one loves the world, the love of the Father is not in him. For all that is in the world, the lust of the flesh and the lust of the eyes and the boastful pride of life, is not from the Father, but is from the world. And the world is passing away, and also its lusts; but the one who does the will of God abides forever. (1 John 2:15-17, NASB)

But when we turn to John's gospel we hear the well-known declaration:

> For God so loved the world, that He gave His only begotten Son, that whoever believes in Him should not perish, but have eternal life. (John 3:16, NASB)

Should we love the world, or not? Is John contradicting himself? *God* loves the world, but *we* are not to love the world? Notice that the same Greek words for "love" (*agapao*) and "world" (*kosmos*) occur in both passages. What is the meaning?

When the apostle John speaks of the "world" it can mean one of at least three things.[2] First, the "world" can refer simply to the material creation into which we and Jesus (John 6:14) were born (John 17:5; 1:10; compare with 1:3-5). The world is created by God and it is still His. This is the world that we can love because God created it for us to care for and to enjoy.

Second, the "world" can refer to humanity capable of believing in God (John 3:16). It is almost a synonym for people in a generic sense, so that Jesus is called the "Savior of the world" (John 4:42). This is the world God loved enough to send His Son to die for. This is the world of non-believers among whom we live and whom we can love with God's love.

Third, the "world" can refer to the present sinful system which is in conflict with God. This is the world which hates Jesus because He calls the selfishness and hurtfulness of people toward each other sin (John 1:9-10; 7:7). Jesus came to enlighten this "world," which is alien (John 8:23) and antagonistic (John 7:7) because it is under evil domination (John 12:31). The disciples and Jesus are *in*, but not *of*, this world (John 17). This is the world that we are not to love—the world that exalts self, that dominates the weak, that promotes a way of life that is godless.

The challenge is living a real life as God intended it to be lived, in the world as we know it, and as God values it. Although this is God's world, it is under the influence of evil to such an extent that the term itself can be used of humanity at war with God. Spiritual agencies have a powerful influence in the world. The demonic world is the background for Jesus' battle for mankind, but there is never any question of His authority. We are safe in this world when we place ourselves in Jesus' care.

Simply put: *We are to love this world which God created, especially the people in it for whom Jesus died, but we are not to love or become part of the world system that now is hostile to God and His efforts to bring it back under His rule.*

The world system tempts us to use others for our own gain, to expend our lives attempting to own more possessions which will only decay. The world system creates godless philosophies that entrap people and turn them against God's ways. The world system will try to get us sidetracked by distractions and temptations. We can also be sidetracked because we want so desperately to fit in, not to be "peculiar" Christians. We can get sidetracked by wanting to build, as Jesus pointed to in the parable, bigger and better stores of material possessions (Luke 12:16-21). It is easy to get sidetracked by the values of this world if we do not hold to our purpose for being in the world.

The ultimate goal of our time here is not to become a success by the definition of this world. The goal is not simply a job, or even our own personal growth and development. The ultimate goal is to become servants of God, in the likeness of Christ, reaching a world that is lost and without hope. God has placed you next door to your neighbors for a purpose. You may be the only Christian your neighbors or coworkers or fellow students ever really get to know—the only person in whom they see the kind of life they desperately want to have.

A sojourner has a "tent maker" mentality. Through the centuries many missionaries have adopted a "tent maker" strategy. Taking the lead from the apostle Paul who supported his missionary outreach in part through his profession of making tents, many missionaries go to foreign lands as professionals. They are able to support themselves financially, and they make inroads to nationals in the business and professional world in ways that traditional missionaries would not be able to do.

I believe that all of us need to have this mentality. Our work enables us to feed ourselves and at the same time enables us to be in a situation where we can develop relationships with people so that we can care for them and provide hope and answers. Businessmen, lawyers, policemen, and teachers, who are first Christians, will be able to go places and develop relationships with people that I will never be able to reach. My overriding purpose, as I train my students, is that each of them—whether their major is business or Bible, education or economics, music or mathematics—will be missionaries wherever God leads them.

Developing a tent maker mentality means two things: *First, we see our work as a means to the end, not the end itself* (Luke 12:16-21, Ephesians 4:28). Many Christians get caught up in their work and forget that we have higher purposes for being here. Sometimes we become so focused on the job that we never even consider how it can be a means to bringing light and salt into the working situation.

Second, our work is part of our commission from God to care for His creation (Genesis 1:28). Work is part of our calling in life. Whatever work we have at any particular time in our lives is an opportunity from

God. Do you take pride in your work, no matter what it is? One of the most powerful witnesses is to be a good worker.

Professor Leland Ryken points out that the Puritan work ethic has been disparaged as the root of a whole range of current problems: the workaholic syndrome, drudgery, competitiveness, worship of success, materialism, and the cult of the self-made person.[3] But in his careful study of the Puritans, whom he calls "worldly saints," Ryken shows that the Puritan attitude toward work is a model for us. They did not make a distinction between sacred and secular occupations because they understood the sanctity of all legitimate kinds of work. They took their occupations as God's calling on their lives, and they held to a moderation in work because success is God's blessing, not something earned.

In Puritan John Milton's epic *Paradise Lost*, no better summary of the Puritan attitude toward work can be found than in Adam's words to Eve,

> Man hath his daily work of body or mind
> Appointed, which declares his dignity,
> And the regard of Heaven on all his ways.[4]

Instead of disparaging them, I have found the Puritans to have one of the most balanced attitudes toward life in this world.

A couple of years ago while I was at a conference in Washington, D.C., with one of my colleagues, we ran across a former student from our school. Although he had studied to go into pastoral ministry, God had opened up a most unexpected door—politics. He had been invited to join the staff of a United States Senator as the Deputy Press Secretary.

He took us on a tour of the Senator's office in the Senate building, took us all around the congressional buildings, and even took us down on the Senate floor. The history, pageantry, and international power invested in those buildings was powerful!

During lunch in the Senate dining room he told us how he had arrived at this position and what he saw for his future. He understood clearly the weighty responsibilities he had in representing the Senator. He understood clearly the power that permeated the office. But he also understood his higher calling. He knew that God had opened up these opportunities not just so that he could develop his own career.

His primary purpose was to have an influence as a Christian on our society. He took his calling from God seriously.

Sojourning Together

Disciples must go into the world together. When Jesus sent out the seventy-two disciples on a preaching mission, He sent them two-by-two. When the mission to the Gentiles was initiated, the Holy Spirit led the church at Antioch to set apart Barnabas and Paul to go out together. There is no place that the community of faith is more necessary than when sojourning in the world.

We saw in the last chapter that *creativity, mentoring, modeling*, and *empathy* are core principles of community discipleship. They are also necessary for disciples sojourning together in the world. To those we add four core principles: *accountability, mutuality, trust*, and *letting go.*

Accountability

Accountability is not always a concept received eagerly. It can sound like control over another person, a position none of us relishes being in.

But the biblical concept of accountability is a positive one. It means helping one another stay on the path toward mature discipleship. It means helping each other stay true to our own commitments. The world offers temptations and distractions to get us off the path. Positive accountability allows us to help each other stay on the path. The writer to the Hebrews declares that we need to consider how we "may spur one another on toward love and good deeds" and how we may "encourage one another" (Hebrews 10:24-25).

Husbands and wives have a natural accountability network. I do quite a bit of speaking to audiences that do not really know me. It is possible for me to exalt myself, to lead people to believe that I am something other than what I am in my daily life. However, my wife goes with me to almost all of my speaking engagements. When I look out on the audience, without a word spoken, Lynne's presence holds me accountable to be real, to speak the truth, to practice what I preach. When a spouse gets off the path, we help each other to be accountable to get back on the right path.

Parents also help their children stay accountable to the right path. Children have not walked this way before. As mature parents we can help them to be safe in a world that has many physical, spiritual, and ethical land mines. This is where the Christian parent must be truly "Christian." In this day of relativity, we cannot know the right way for our children to walk in the world unless we are clear about what it means to be a real Christian. If we are going to hold our children accountable to the right path, we have to know what it is, and we have to be traveling it ourselves.

Accountability helps us to remain consistent. Preachers often make the apostle Peter the target of mockery because in his early years as a disciple he was inconsistent. But Peter is also the model of a person who *learned how to become consistent.* A key to his consistency was accountability: He was accountable to Jesus, to the other apostles, and later to Paul.

Consistency in our developing walk with God in this world will grow as we learn to be accountable to others. Have you allowed yourself to become vulnerable to the point where you need others? If we are going to remain consistently faithful to Jesus while we sojourn in this world we must develop an accountability network with other sojourners. Try incorporating the following suggestions for developing healthy accountability.

First, acquire a habit of transparency and confessing your sins and weaknesses to one another (James 5:16). This requires a great deal of confidence in the other person. The person will need to be able to carry your burden with you without it becoming too heavy for him or her to share with you (Galatians 6:1-5). Also you will have to have confidence that the other person is mature enough to allow you to grow to overcome the problems you may have. Sometimes they hold it against you. Be wise in understanding the person.

Then allow the other person to help hold you accountable. Allow the person to check up on you periodically. I suggest that you set regular meeting times. However, I believe that the best way a person holds us accountable is silently. When I have opened my life to another person about an issue, all I have to do is see them and I am reminded of what I need to do to stay on the right path. Because, of course, the point is to internalize your commitment to living a pure, committed life. Letting someone else hold you accountable to commitment is similar to seeing a stop sign on the road. Without a sound, the stop sign reminds me of my responsibility as a driver. I can disobey, but if I am serious about my driving ethic, I will stop. Your fellow sojourner is a silent test of your integrity in the world.

Second, allow others appropriate authority over your life—helping you to say no, calling you on phoniness, keeping you honest. I believe that God has given me a responsibility to minister, so I have a difficult time saying no to people who ask me to speak at their church or conference. Another less noble reason is that I like for people to like me, and if I say no they might be displeased with me. So sometimes I say yes when I shouldn't.

Therefore, I almost never give a *yes* or *no* to my calendar without checking with my wife. I have given her veto rights. We talk through each decision, but I have given her authority. I believe that this is an appropriate way of allowing her to hold me accountable to the kind of schedule I really want.

This works in another way with my children. As with Lynne, when they come to where I am speaking, or when they read what I have written, their presence holds me accountable not to stretch the truth for an effect. It keeps me real in both public and private when my daughters are with me.

Third, always meet regularly with one brother or sister. Invite that person into both your public and private life. One person I met with for a while had a marvelous testimony among his Christian friends. But when he was at work, where he was vice president of his company, he had a ruthless way of dealing with people. He could mercilessly cut down a person verbally in front of other workers. He demanded performance from his employees that was completely unreasonable. This man needed to be confronted about the dichotomy between his performance at church and at the office.

Mutuality

Mutuality—the interdependence we have with other believers—declares that we are in process together as we live out our lives in this world. This requires an attitude which recognizes that we are equals in many ways because it provides the opportunity for us to learn from each other's strengths and mistakes.

In spite of our inadequacies, in spite of our lack of full maturity, the Lord desires to use us in the lives of others. The help we provide others will not be perfect, in the same way that the help we receive from them will not be perfect. Regardless, we need each other.

Just prior to the disastrous denials by Peter, Jesus revealed that

Satan was going to sift Peter. However, Jesus went on to say that once Peter had recovered from this time of personal defeat he was to strengthen his brothers (Luke 22:31-34).

Peter then experienced such a crushing, humiliating defeat in denying Jesus that he could have been too ashamed ever to lift his head in service again. The other disciples could easily have refused to rely upon him again in any leadership position. The consequences for sin and a stricter discipline for leaders in the church are both real; nonetheless, Jesus restored Peter by commissioning him to turn and strengthen his brothers. It was because he understood the instinct to betray Jesus that Peter could effectively strengthen the whole early church as it went through vicious persecution. This incident teaches us that we must concentrate on investing in others in spite of our inadequacies and/or immaturity. It is as we learn from our own trials and failures that we can be used to help others in their own difficulties.

The following points have been helpful to me when developing mutuality:

First, consistency in our personal life and walk with the Lord is made more real when the fact grips us that the strength of others depends upon our consistency. Yes, you may have failed. Yes, you may be inadequate. Yes, you may not yet be fully mature. But your brothers and sisters in Christ need you!

Second, don't fall into the trap of comparison. Comparison tends to rob us of the uniqueness that God has given each of us. I pointed out earlier that when we compare ourselves with others, someone always either loses or wins, depending upon our particular insecurities. Comparison can paralyze us because we think that everyone else does it better. Comparison can give us an inaccurate estimate of ourselves if we aren't honest—either too high or too low.

Third, allow others to be restored in the same way that the Lord restores you. Sometimes we hold failure against people because we may not think that they deserve to be restored yet. We each want forgiveness and restoration. Give to others the same grace that you want.

Fourth, be careful of the "tug of war" syndrome. In a tug of war over needs, we continually seek to have others take care of our own needs and interests. When we feel another person tugging to have their needs met, we tug back even harder. They feel us tug, so they dig in and tug harder yet, thus initiating the ongoing tug of war.

A servant's heart seeks to meet needs. I challenge young engaged couples for the six months prior to their wedding never to ask for their own needs to be met. Instead, they are to ask only what the other person's needs are, and how they can meet those needs. If they are faithful to that commitment, they each will have their own needs met without ever asking! But if their own needs aren't met, it may be an indication that their future partner will not meet their needs after the wedding. This helps them develop a pattern of life that breaks the tug of war that plagues so many marriages.

Trust

We must have trust at the heart of our relationships because our walk in the world will lead us into circumstances that require us to rely on others and God. Sight does not always work.

Consider the well-known story of Peter walking out to Jesus on the water (Matthew 14:22-33). Peter was fine on the water until he looked at his circumstances ("saw the wind," verse 30). As soon as Peter looked at his circumstances and took his eyes off Jesus, he found himself in trouble. Notice that Jesus did not condemn Peter for getting out of the boat. Jesus only later corrected him for his "little faith" (verse 31).

The circumstances we face from day to day will change, but the one constancy we have in this life is Jesus. Although we cannot literally see Jesus, as Peter did, we *can* rely upon His presence. He will be there with us whatever we encounter, to help us make the right decisions, give us courage in the face of opposition, or comfort us in sorrowful situations. Since Jesus dwells in our hearts (Ephesians 3:17), through eyes of faith we need to focus on His presence in our lives instead of becoming unsettled by circumstances we have never encountered before. This is a key ingredient for a Christlike lifestyle in this world.

How do we live by faith above our circumstances?

First, practice the presence of Jesus. Learn to open your conscious attention to Jesus everywhere you go and to develop a line of communication with Him in all of your circumstances. This does take commitment and practice because we naturally focus on the people and circumstances right before our eyes and on our own emotions as we encounter them.

Second, remember that your circumstances are not the measure of Jesus' love for you. Jesus will never leave you, and He never loves you less, even though our circumstances cause us to doubt Him. Life in this world is hard. You and I will face hardships, illness, even persecution. The health and wealth message of some preachers suggests that your material and temporal successes are an indication of the blessing of God in your life. But the testimony of biblical figures and Christians throughout history belies that message. Even as Jesus' purpose in life was to suffer the cross for us, we have been called to suffer for His sake (Philippians 1:29)—whether the suffering comes directly from persecution for our faith, or from engaging in the spiritual warfare of this life, or from living in a world that is still under the curse of sin and death. Jesus never loves us less, even though circumstances seem to indicate that He is far away.

Third, open yourself up to experiencing Jesus' power, presence, and love in the most difficult circumstances. As I've said, circumstances are not the measure of Jesus' love for us. We know that He is near, and we can call on Him to give us strength to overcome, grace to learn, and love to serve in every circumstance.

Our daughter, Michelle, had serious bouts of illness from the time she was a baby. One time when she was four, she developed a serious case of flu. Her temperature kept rising steadily. By midnight it had reached 105 degrees. We called the nurse on duty several times that night, but she told us just to keep her cool and quiet.

That night Lynne slept on the floor of the bathroom with Michelle because it was the coolest spot in the house. About two in the morning, Michelle finally quit crying and was quiet the rest of the night—but the next day Michelle would not wake up.

In a hospital emergency room we got the terrifying news: A spinal tap revealed Michelle had spinal meningitis. They immediately started filling her intravenously with antibiotics. But the doctor took me aside and said that it had advanced so rapidly that there was nothing they could do. "Mr. Wilkins," he said, "we're too late. Michelle won't live through the night."

Lynne had stayed home with our younger daughter, so I had to call and tell her. She immediately rushed to the hospital.

I remember sitting there, alone with Michelle, crying and saying, "Lord, I know that You love her even more than we do. And we trust her with You. But," I cried out, "we're not through with her yet!"

When Lynne got to the hospital Michelle was quietly lying there. Lynne kissed her and then we stood holding each other, trying to comfort each other.

Later that night we stood over Michelle's bed, holding hands, and asked for God to spare her for a while. We sang songs to her. We sang one little chorus from a John Denver song that Michelle loved to walk around the house singing. It went something like this:

> I'll walk in the rain by your side,
> I'll cling to the warmth of your tiny hand.
> I'll do anything, to help you understand,
> I'll love you more than anybody can.[5]

As we sang, there was suddenly the slightest movement in one of her little fingers. Then a flicker of her eyelids. Before long she opened her eyes. She screamed out in pain because of the swelling in her brain and spinal column.

A little later the doctor consulted with us and said, "I can't explain this, but it looks like Michelle is going to survive." He seemed bewildered.

"But," he went on, "the swelling is so bad that she is going to have permanent brain damage. She may never again function in a normal way."

Michelle couldn't walk for several weeks. She had to learn to walk and talk all over again. But since that time she has recovered completely. Miraculously. She has gone on to be an outstanding student, graduating from high school and college with highest honors. And she has such fine balance that she has become an excellent surfer! As little as she was, Michelle remembers what happened. She has told us many times that she considers her life to be a gift from God.

Other situations have not turned out so wonderfully from our human perspective. But like other Christians before us, we have learned how to let circumstances drive us into greater trust in God. We rely on the truth that Jesus is with us in every circumstance, that He has power over all circumstances, and that He never stops loving us—even though it doesn't seem like it in the middle of the hardest time.

Focus on intimacy with Jesus instead of circumstances, and then you will be able to trust Him no matter what comes your way.

Letting Go

From the moment of birth we progressively let our children go. A biological cord is cut which is prophetic of later parental cords that must be cut. Since the ultimate goal of our parental task is to help our children be healthy adults who are growing in Christ, we are simply a means to that end. We provide support, guidance, and a model of how to live in the world. But eventually *we have to let them go.*

This means, in part, giving our children increasing responsibility for their own lives. As they approach maturity, they gain both independence and responsibility. The measure of their maturity is often found in how they balance both. At times we find that we don't always agree with the paths our children take in later life, yet if we trust their motives and integrity, we must trust them to take that path, even when we don't agree.

This same process is also true in our relations with other believers. We have to let others go to walk with Jesus. In another famous scene between Jesus and Peter, Jesus turned Peter loose to care for Jesus' sheep (John 21:15-19). Three times Jesus questioned Peter's love for Him; three times Peter acknowledges his love for Jesus, and three times Jesus instructs Peter to care for His sheep. Among the many intriguing elements of this story, we see that Jesus restored Peter in front of the other disciples after his tragic three denials, loosed Peter to public service, and also predicted his martyr's death (John 21:18-19).

But as is so often the case with our dear friend Peter, he overstepped his bounds. He turned and asked about the role and fate of the beloved disciple. Jesus, in essence, says it is none of Peter's business. As Jesus turned Peter loose, so Peter had to trust God for others.

Learning to help others grow in Christ means, to a certain extent, that we must let others go to walk with God in this world and be ultimately responsible to Him, not to us.[6]

This "Serious" Business

As we conclude this section, I would like to give one principle that has helped bring balance to my life as a growing Christian: *Take God's calling upon your life with absolute seriousness—but don't take yourself too seriously.*

In another classic passage, Jesus declared Peter to be a "rock." He said Peter's potential for ministry as an apostle was uniquely significant for Jesus' church (Matthew 16:13-20), and He gave Peter the keys to the kingdom of heaven. Peter would indeed exercise an incredibly important role in the establishment of the church by carrying the gospel to his Jewish people, to the despised Samaritans, and to the hated Gentiles, just as Jesus ordained.[7]

But note what happened immediately after this. Jesus announced the necessity of going to the cross (Matthew 16:21), and it was Peter who tried to hinder Him. Now Jesus called Peter a "stumbling block" because Peter had set his mind on human interests, not on God's (Matthew 16:21-23).[8] Without consistency of character, Peter the rock became Peter the stumbling stone.

What was true for Peter is true for us: It is supremely important for each of us to know our God-given potential in this life and then focus upon maximizing all that to which God has called us. Yet we cannot become so carried away with our importance that we overstep our responsibilities. For then our passion for living borders on arrogance, which is a counterfeit of godly confidence. Confidence in God is simply recognizing what God has given us to do and doing it in His strength . . . *and no more*!

There is an important principle here, understanding who we are as God's servants in this world. *We are both indispensable and dispensable*. Remember these simple foundational truths:

- Know yourself, know your gifts, know that God desires to use you in a particular way. The life and ministry to which God has called you is unique and you are unique. There is no one who can do it quite like you.
- Recognize that God's purposes go beyond any one of us. I love to remind myself that if God can talk through Balaam's donkey, of course He can talk through me! If I don't function as God designed me, I can be set aside.

Even though you and I are absolutely crucial to God's plans, the kingdom does not depend upon any one of us. God's purposes go beyond any one of us. God is the architect of life and our relationships, not us. Our ability to serve others is dependent upon our openness to God's work in our life.

Finally, remember Paul's admonition to a church living in a pagan society, "Follow my example, as I follow the example of Christ"

(1 Corinthians 11:1). As we are salt and light, as we walk the narrow path, as we love and provide hope to the world, we become the living example for others to follow as we travel home to be with God.

PART THREE

TOWARD A NEW VISION OF DISCIPLESHIP AND SPIRITUALITY

CHAPTER ELEVEN

When Love Attacks Your Heart

The effect of a rending of heart
is perseverance in the virtues and
the many-coloured unity of a beautiful life.
BERNARD OF CLAIRVAUX (CIRCA. A.D. 1140)[1]

■

At this very moment, each one of us has a heart condition. Some of us are only too aware of the condition of our *physical* heart. But are we aware that we each have a *spiritual* heart condition as well?

The medical industry invests millions of dollars each year in an attempt to evaluate and attend to the condition of the physical heart. But how do we go about attending to our spiritual heart? I find that many people do know that the condition of their spiritual heart is unhealthy, but they don't know what to do about it.

How would you evaluate your heart? Healthy? Hurting? Hardened? In chapter seven we discussed briefly how the Holy Spirit's work in our lives includes the transformation of our spiritual heart. Here we want to consider how to heal broken hearts, how to strengthen hurting hearts, and how to guard healthy hearts.

How Is Your Heart?

The heart is a fascinating thing. The *material heart* is the center of our physical life. It keeps our life's blood circulating, it pounds furiously when we are afraid or when we are in love. It beats away millions of times during a lifetime without our ever giving it a thought, but in a moment, when it flutters or stops, our whole world is focused on its few inches of muscle.

The *spiritual heart* is the center of our spiritual, emotional, and psychological life. The spiritual heart is where I experience life's joys and sorrows, where I connect deeply with my wife and children, where I ponder my existence, and where I encounter God.

Each of us has experienced things in life that have affected our spiritual hearts. We may have been hurt or abused, so we have hardened our heart to prevent being hurt again. A hardened heart protects us, but that is not the way a heart is supposed to be. We may have chosen to steal or lie or hurt others to get ahead, so we have hardened our heart in order not to feel conscience or guilt. We may even pride ourselves on our hard heart, *but that is not the way a heart is supposed to be.*

Through many of the circumstances of my early life, I can see now that as a young person I had developed a heart that was as cold and hard as stone. I could lie and not be bothered. I could hurt people and not have a twinge of conscience. I could steal, even from a church, and laugh at their stupidity for leaving cash in sight.

I also now know that I had been hurt by some of life's circumstances; in my immaturity I hardened my heart so that I would not be hurt again. I was protecting myself, but I was also developing a heart that couldn't receive love and affection and couldn't give it either. That is not the way a heart is supposed to be! I was a person in need, but I didn't even know it.

Then I went into the Army. As you might expect, my heart became even more hardened. Training a young man for combat does not include teaching him how to be sensitive and vulnerable! As I went to Vietnam I was a hard young man at the age of nineteen. My arrogance was encouraged when I became part of a cocky and efficient combat group, the 173rd Airborne Infantry Brigade. I had been trained to be a war machine, and I did that well. I was point man for my squad and platoon.

Then my life was forever altered. One day while we were on a typical search-and-destroy mission we came out of the jungle into a clearing with a little rice paddy and a small river running beside it. Walking along the river I happened to look down into it, and just then I saw two eyes looking back at me from the water. At the same instant I saw the muzzle of a rifle come out of the water and point toward me. It all happened so quickly that I don't remember the rest of the details, but I found myself a few minutes later going into the river to recover the man's body and two other bodies. We weren't sure whether they had intended to ambush us, or whether they were surprised by our coming out of the jungle and had tried to hide.

That was just one of many days when that sort of thing happened. But that day stands out more than any other because of its effect on me. It was the first time I had looked a person in the eyes and killed him. Yet I carried on as though it was normal. An American reporter from the Associated Press was traveling with us at the time, and he took a picture of me to circulate in the newspapers at home. There I stood with my foot on the dead, young soldier's chest, my weapon pointed down at him. *I was the cocky, cold-hearted war machine . . . .*

Until that night on guard duty. We had settled into a defensive perimeter that night somewhere in the jungle. It was pitch black. No moon. But I remember the stars being brilliant. As I sat there, listening for an attack from the enemy, I thought of that young man, probably no older than I was and quite likely even younger. He probably had a family at home worrying about him. He probably had a girlfriend waiting for their future to begin. He had all of the same hopes and dreams I did. Yet in one brief second, I had taken his life away from him. Sure, that was the way of war. But I started to cry. I cried like a baby. And the more I thought, the more I cried.

During that hour on guard duty in the jungle of Vietnam in my nineteenth year of life, God gently, firmly attacked my cold, hard heart. A crack occurred in that hard heart, which over the next months and years widened and deepened so that when the time came, my heart was open to hear the message about Jesus' love for me, a message that resulted in my receiving a new heart.

That night when God attacked my heart, the war machine was changed. I continued to be effective. I continued to walk point for the next four months. But I was different. I was more focused on people. I loved my men, and I came to have a passionate love for the Vietnamese people, which lasts to this day. In my mind's eye I can still see their pain-wracked, yet open and wonderfully caring faces, especially the children and their smiles and laughter in that hell of war.

I wasn't created by God to have a hard heart, and neither were you. But life has a way of affecting all of us. Like me, you may have been so hurt by people that you have a heart that, right now, is afraid to open up to anyone. Or you may have hardened your heart toward God because you believe that He has treated you unfairly. You might be so intent upon getting what you want from people that you have hardened yourself not to feel anything toward them.

But that is not the way a heart is supposed to be. Christian discipleship—growth in Christ—starts first with your heart. God wants to restore your heart to the place where you can love again. He wants to help you develop a heart that is healthy and whole.

The Beginning of the Revolution

The turning point for the world occurred two thousand years ago. The world then, like the world today, had a hard heart. It was intent upon its own pleasures. It was wracked by war and pain and crime as people hurt each other in their ego-driven need to dominate.

Even within God's chosen people, the children of Israel, the message of redemption from God through the prophets was muffled. Dominated by foreign powers for centuries, they were oppressed and hurt and angry. Tired of waiting for God's help, some fought for themselves. Others gave up on God completely and went looking for other earthly pleasures or answers to life's questions. Various wise men and teachers and priests overlaid God's message with their own religious answers. And so the heart of the people of God became hard.

Into that condition of heart, Jesus came with a revolution. Not a revolution of weapons or politics or anarchy, but a revolution of the heart. He attacked their hearts. And He attacked by loving men and women just as He found them in their everyday world. Then He called them to follow Him to learn more of this revolutionary love—to join Him in loving others.

This was not the norm in Israel when it came to master-disciple relationships. Normally other things were at the center of this kind of relationship, whether it was study, teaching, baptism, or religious ceremony such as with the Pharisees.

But Jesus' relationship with His disciples was centered in love. During His final night with them, just hours away from His impending betrayal, trial, and crucifixion, He said:

> "A new commandment I give to you, that you love one another, even as I have loved you, that you also love one another. By this all people will know that you are my disciples, if you have love for one another." (John 13:34-35, NASB)

"Love" in the New Testament is a specific term for a uniquely biblical orientation toward relationships. This orientation is found in two verses which we know well. In fact, some of us know them so well they lose their impact.

Listen, as though for the first time, to the revolutionary nature of God's love:

> For God so loved the world, that He gave His only begotten Son, that whoever believes in Him should not perish, but have eternal life. (John 3:16, NASB)

Listen also to Paul's powerful understanding of God's love for us:

> But God demonstrates His own love toward us, in that while we were yet sinners, Christ died for us. (Romans 5:8, NASB)

The cure for a hard heart, Jesus declares, is love. But what does that mean? I love my wife, I love my daughters, I love my mom, I even love my wife's cat, Maui. I love my new surfboard. These are very different kinds of love. What does it mean to say that Jesus loves me and that I am to love others? We must understand clearly the difference between the world's definitions of love and the biblical definition. We hear many different perspectives on love all around us.

The World's Love Versus God's Love

Everywhere we turn, on television, in magazines, in movies, people talk about love. In the world, love is described in some of the following ways:

- Love is a strong feeling of affection.
- Love is a feeling of brotherhood and goodwill.
- Love can be equated with infatuation.
- Love is regularly portrayed as a strong, passionate, sexual attraction, not far from lust.
- Love can mean gaining benefit from someone or something else, as a plant loves the shade.
- "Love means never having to say you're sorry"—a most pathetic definition!

- Love is often understood as a self-gratifying relationship with someone or something else, especially a status symbol: I love my car, I love my new job, I love where I live.

But we find in the actions of Jesus a unique kind of love. A definition of Jesus' kind of love, which I suggested earlier in chapter seven, is this:

> Love is an unconditional commitment to an imperfect person, a commitment I give myself to in order to bring the relationship to God's intended purpose.

Consider that definition with me for a while, and think about your own heart and your own relationships.

I know a pastor who announced to his board and his church that he was divorcing his wife of twenty-five years and that he wanted to remain as pastor. He said that she was an alcoholic and that she was mentally abusive. He said that he was divorcing her because he wanted to be happy with his life. Besides, she was holding back his ministry. He said he didn't love her anymore. He wanted to experience a life that was filled with happiness, and he could not find that in his marriage. So he divorced her, discovered another woman that he says he now *really* loves, and has married her to begin a whole new life.

On the other hand, I remember my wife and her parents often talking about the pastor under whose ministry she was raised. Although I knew him only briefly before he passed away, he has set for me a standard of love that exemplifies Jesus' love.

This man and his wife planted the church in which my wife was raised. Everything seemed to be going along well for the couple and for the church. But then the pastor's wife developed mental problems. It got so severe that she was virtually incapacitated. She would perform the most bizarre scenes. One day the pastor came home for lunch and his wife had taken all of the china and kitchen utensils out on the front lawn and was pretending to have a meal for the neighbors.

People would often say to the pastor, "Why don't you just leave her, put her away, get a divorce? She is sick, and she is just holding back your ministry." His response to them was, "How can I? I must love her with the same love that Jesus loved me, and Jesus gave His life for me."

I can't be the final judge of the right or wrong of either of these pastors. But I can say that the second pastor was attempting to go by the biblical example of love that we see in Jesus—*an unconditional commitment to an imperfect person, a commitment I give myself to in order to bring the relationship to God's intended purpose.*

Earlier we saw that in our new life in Christ our heart is regenerated to be like God's heart. And now we have available to us an endless supply of love from God. Through the power of the Holy Spirit you and I now are able to love and to be loved with Jesus' love.

Diagnosing Hardness of Heart

Although God broke through my hard heart over twenty-five years ago, I still struggle with a hard heart. In the circumstances of my daily life, I must keep careful watch over my heart because of its tendency to harden again.

How Does a Heart Harden?

People live with sin that they keep hidden, thinking they can even hide from God. But as long as we live with sin in our lives, we are hardening our heart to the Spirit who is trying both to convict us and set us free. While we live in this condition, holding on to sin, we continually harden our heart.

I can see my heart harden as I let anger dominate my life. I become angry when I see people take advantage of other people. When I see our society increasingly slide into depravity I can become angry at the leaders within our culture who perpetuate that depravity in the name of freedom. Whatever we might think of the issues involved, if I am not careful my anger can cause my heart to harden when I let it dominate my life. It can turn into pridefulness when I want to become the all-knowing policeman for God who straightens everyone out.

I see clearly in my own life that my heart hardens the quickest when I close myself off from people as I become critical and cynical. I stand back and find fault with people. In my critical cynicism I then isolate myself into my own little hard-hearted, self-righteous world.

You and I can also harden our hearts because of circumstances that pressure us and hurt us from the outside. Each of you reading these words has been hurt in life. We often try to protect ourselves by hardening our heart against the hurt so that we don't experience the pain.

We can also harden our heart by turning to fearfulness, arrogance, or bitterness as means of protecting ourselves. Let's look at the effect each of these has on us.

Fear. Fear can be an appropriate emotional response which is triggered by a real threat or problem. It can help us to respond effectively. But fear can also be inappropriate. It can produce anxiety, worry, panic, and a host of other emotions.[2] We can become so fearful of life and our lack of ability to handle it that we harden our heart.

Arrogance. Arrogance is another condition that contributes toward hardness of heart. Arrogance is an overawareness of, or an overrated perception of, one's abilities. It distances us from reality and from normal relationships with people because we think so highly of ourselves that we lose an accurate perception of ourselves and those around us. When we have an accurate perception of ourselves, our abilities and giftedness, and when we are sure of God's leading in our lives, we can approach life with confidence. But arrogance is a counterfeit of confidence because it usually comes at the expense of other people, and it can mask doubts about ourselves. It can also mask anger and conceit.

Bitterness. Another serious spiritual heart condition is bitterness. "Life isn't fair," we often hear. I can see the faces of countless numbers of young people who say, "Why did my parents have to get a divorce? Why did their messing up their lives have to mess up mine?" These are difficult questions to answer, but the tragedy is watching these young people harden their hearts as a result. Perhaps a young father hardens his heart to his wife and God as he buries his firstborn child, or a mother hardens her heart as she sees her children turn their backs on her, "after all I've done for them."

Saying No to God

The most serious way in which our heart hardens is when we say *no* to the Holy Spirit's influence in our lives, when we want our way instead of God's way, so our heart hardens against God's leading. We intentionally or unintentionally close ourselves off from God's love coming to our help. This can actually lead to sin as a person, instead of turning to God for help, shuts God out.

The tragedy is that each time we say no to God our heart hardens a bit more. It often happens in such a subtle manner that we don't see the long-term effects. My wife recently told me that she saw my heart hardening because I was so intent upon straightening out the wrongs I saw around me that I wasn't at the same time loving people. A hardened heart cannot put another person's needs ahead of its own.

As Christians, we must be starkly honest with ourselves because we can so easily conceal a hard heart. One way a hard heart can be masked is behind external acts of religion. There are many people in churches today with hard hearts. They regularly attend church and appear to be religious, but their hearts are hardened to God and to His people. A hard heart can also be masked behind glitzy performances, whether the performance is preaching, singing, praying, or serving.

Religious heart diseases too often go unseen by the one who has them. Yet they eat away at our spiritual health even when they are masked by religious activities which, ironically, only feed the disease instead of healing us.

Curing Spiritual Heart Conditions

I'd like to recommend the following help for a hard heart.

First, open your heart to God. Talk openly to Him about your hurt, your strong-minded plans to advance yourself over others, your fears, your temptations. He wants to enter into a relationship with you exactly the way you are right now. Our heart must be open before Him so that He can apply the necessary healing. What is your particular heart condition? If your hardness of heart is caused by sin, *confess it.* If it is caused by hurt, *open yourself up to God's healing and comfort.* If it is caused by bitterness, *acknowledge the source of pain.* In all cases, allow God to walk with you through it, even if you don't understand all of the reasons for the suffering.

Second, allow God's love to penetrate deeply into your heart to bring healing. In the earliest days of my Christian life I drove an old Volkswagen van. I had Jesus stickers all over that van, but one that always brought a smile to my face was inside the van, just above the windshield. It said: "Smile, God Loves You."

I understood deep within my heart that Jesus came into this world to love us in a personal way. The reason I could smile now, even as a young man who had been so hard and callous, was because Jesus loved me. The God of the universe loved me!—and that brought an understanding of who I was and the purpose of life that God had given me. His love has been the health of my heart ever since. His endless love has given me a source from which I can give love to those around me.

One of the serious dangers of being in a Christian setting is that Jesus becomes simply a religious figure to us. We can easily lose the sense that He is indeed present in our everyday lives. But if Jesus is real, if He is who He says He is, if He has truly been raised from the dead, then He loves you and me this very day. We need to experience that love as we consider the God of this universe who came into our world to love us.

Many people have difficulty with this concept. Let me offer a prescription that I have used myself, which has been of immediate help to many people.

Go off by yourself to a quiet place. Meditate upon the verses we mentioned earlier.

> For God so loved the world, that He gave His only begotten Son, so that everyone who believes in Him should not perish, but have eternal life. (John 3:16, NASB)

> But God demonstrates His own love toward us, in that while we were yet sinners, Christ died for us. (Romans 5:8, NASB)

As you quietly dwell upon those verses, personalize them:

> "God so loved *me*."
> "God demonstrates His own love toward *me* . . . Christ died for *me*."

Accept these truths deeply into your own life. The work of God from eternity had you in view. He wants His love to soften your heart so that you are more alive and human. Talk to Jesus. Tell Him of your hurt. Tell Him of your sin. Tell Him of your emptiness. Let His love come into your heart.

When Lynne and I have an argument, especially a deeply hurtful one, I harden my heart to her. If she has hurt me, I harden myself by not allowing her into my life. I keep her away from the deepest parts of my heart. The only way of reversing that is to quietly review our lives together, looking at her commitment and dedication toward me. And then I have to open back up to her, knowing that she could hurt me again. But our marriage will not grow if I maintain a hard heart.

The same goes for you and Jesus. Review His love for you, open yourself up to Him, and allow Him to enter into the deepest recesses of your life with His love.

Spiritual Pacemaker

Next, I suggest that you insert a spiritual pacemaker. During open heart surgery a pacemaker is often inserted for the daily well-being of the patient. A pacemaker is an electrical source that makes the heart beat at a predetermined rate. It helps the physical heart do what it can't do on its own.

The jolt to our spiritual heart that you and I need is to experience God's love, and then have that love as a daily source of stimulation. Jesus' love is not something to acknowledge once and then leave aside. His love can be a regulating force in our lives every day. When we receive Jesus into our hearts, His love enables us to love in a way that we cannot do on our own.

When my wife and I had been married about two or three years, she asked me, "Why don't you tell me that you love me more often?"

In all honesty I remember telling her, "I told you I loved you when I married you."

Of course, that was a witless thing to say. And Lynne let me know it! She said, "When you tell me you love me, I'm reminded how important I am to you. And when I'm that important to you, you become more important in everything I do. How important do you want to be in my life?"

From that point on I began to tell her every day that I loved her!

I recommend that you do a special study of God's love in the Bible. In many study Bibles you will find a topical index. Look up the topic "Love." Under it you will find subtopics like "Love of Christ," "Love of God," "Love to Christ," and "Love to God." Look up two or three verses every day. You'll begin to immerse yourself in what biblical love is all about, and you will begin to understand more clearly than ever before how Jesus' love can be your spiritual pacemaker.

Frequent Checkups

If you want to keep growing in God's love, I recommend frequent checkups to see how you're doing. We need to examine our spiritual heart on a regular basis, especially asking ourselves some tough questions. The most important place to start is to examine our motives.

Why do you do what you do? Are your actions regularly influenced by what you will get out of it? This can be a harsh examination because all of us are still influenced by selfishness this side of heaven. But if self-centeredness *dominates* why we do what we do, then we are developing a hard heart. We need to be starkly honest with ourselves.

Not too long ago I got a call from one of our alumni who was pastoring a small church in the Pacific Northwest. He called to get advice about how to deal with a problem in his church. He was at loggerheads with the church board. They didn't like his style of ministry, and they were swaying the people to their side. Now this young pastor was basically standing alone against the church.

As he recounted the issues, I sided with the pastor. But as he went on, I heard something else in the situation. Then he asked my advice.

"Dave (not his real name), you probably were right about the issues at first," I replied. "But I think the real problem now is that you don't love your people."

"What do you mean? Of course I love them. Look at the sacrifices I've made for them!"

But as we talked more, he came to see a piece of the truth he'd avoided. Somewhere along the way he had fallen out of love with them and he'd lost his love commitment to them. Now he was simply giving a pastoral performance, day in and day out.

The problem surfaces time and time again. I believe that the number one problem of pastors and pastoral staff in the local church is that they don't love their people. Instead, they fall prey to the disease of performance. They try to lead by performing well. They try to gain attention by highly visible, even spectacular performances. They try to impress their people by how much they know, and how much they do. They try to bully and even try to manipulate their people by suggesting that they are the only ones who really know the Bible because they have been to seminary, and they know Greek!

I have spoken to many pastors over the years who have had this very condition of heart. As they encounter opposition and disappointment, it's all too easy to lose the love for their people. Their people become the enemy, and the life of the pastor becomes a "me against them" experience.

But I hasten to add that the same goes for the people of a church. When a pastor is doing well, the people love him. But I have heard pastors described in the most hateful ways when they are not in line with the desires of the people.

A hard heart will show itself in selfishness and pride. We need to examine our hearts regularly to see whether hardness is developing.

Regular Exercise

Finally, your heart will become healthier as you get regular exercise. A few years ago I experienced an irregular heartbeat. I'd wake up in the middle of the night with my heart pounding furiously but irregularly. At times it felt like it was going to stop beating altogether. I went to the doctor for a complete checkup, after which he told me that my heart was pretty healthy for a person in his mid-forties. But my heart needed more exercise.

That was the last thing I wanted to hear. I was already too busy and under too much stress. But he told me that the busier I was and the more stress I experienced, the more I needed to take time to give my heart exercise. So over the last five years I've developed a regular habit of going for a four-to-five-mile walk and jog on the beach every day I'm home. At first I exercised dutifully, but now I exercise joyfully. I enjoy the physical stimulation, but this daily exercise now also allows me to enjoy God's creation, to clear my mind of pressing concerns, and to focus on the bigger picture of what I should be doing with my life.

That daily habit is good for my physical heart, and it gives me an example of what's good for my spiritual heart as well. The most important exercise for our spiritual heart is to love. The harder our heart, the more we need to give ourselves in a commitment of love to the people God has brought into our lives. I often don't feel like caring for people when my heart is hard. And this is to my detriment because then I miss the rewards I receive when I give myself to my wife, children, or students. But as I give myself to others I am allowing God to love through me. My heart slowly begins to soften, and I am able to enjoy my relationships and my calling in life.

Teresa of Avila was an extremely influential Christian woman of the sixteenth century, especially because of her rare ability to help men and women understand the love of God. Her mystical experience of the love of God was a tangible reality in her most difficult circumstances. Some have been critical of her religious ecstasies. But Teresa's experience was not something confined to her prayer closet. Teresa's mystical experiences of God's love were balanced by a daily demonstration of love poured out to those around her. For Teresa of Avila, love meant servanthood in its purest form. She declared:

> Let everyone understand that real love of God does not consist in tear-shedding, nor in that sweetness and tenderness for which we usually long, just because they console us, but in serving God in justice, fortitude of soul, and humility.[3]

Teresa would tell us that the love of God is experienced most tangibly on a daily basis as we love God by serving others.

I recommend that you develop a regular pattern of life in which you allow Jesus to help you love others. Allow Him into your consciousness in each circumstance of your life by talking to Him, by consulting with Him about the people and tasks you encounter each day. Ask Him to help you make decisions in your relationships so that His guidance can spill over from your life to others.

For your first exercise of love try this: Think of your closest relationship, and think also of the relationship that gives you the most pain (it could be the same one). As you prepare yourself for the next encounter with both of those persons, memorize 1 Corinthians 13:4-8. This is like a stretching exercise to warm you up for the real exercise of loving them. Take to heart these words and ask the Spirit to make them real in you:

> Love is patient, love is kind.
> It does not envy, it does not boast, it is not proud.
> It is not rude, it is not self-seeking, it is not easily angered, it
> keeps no record of wrongs.
> Love does not delight in evil but rejoices with the truth.
> It always protects, always trusts, always hopes, always perseveres.
> Love never fails.

Keep these verses in mind as you interact with these persons. You don't have to gush with pretended niceness because God's love is an action. Look for ways to exercise kindness when you don't feel kind. How can you avoid being rude, even if the other person is rude to you? How can you best protect this person from hurt? You can use these verses as a practical guide for a daily exercise of love.

As you allow God to love you with His kind of love, you will be able to understand how to love others in the same way. Our first attempts may be awkward and less than perfect. But the more you give yourself diligently to this daily exercise, the more your heart will be strengthened so you can speak and act out of a heart filled with God's love.

Here are some practical exercises that have helped me learn how to love in all of my relationships.

Give yourself to others, not just your duties and responsibilities. Relationships become cold and lifeless when they are based only on duty. Husbands and fathers, you may have fulfilled your duties to your wife or children, but have you given yourself? Take time to talk with your wife as she fixes dinner. You might even help her. Give a Saturday morning to ride bikes with your son or daughter. Look for ways to give yourself.

Reverse the dynamic of the relationship from taking to giving. Ask most people why they want to get married, and they will usually describe their reasons in terms of getting. "I will become more fulfilled in marriage," one might say. Or, "I've always wanted to have a husband and children and a home of my own." These are not necessarily bad, but marriage as God intended it is a relationship of giving ourselves to another for his or her enrichment. Reverse the orientation, so that you engage in your relationships to give.

Enter into the other's experiences of life. This is where those two important words I learned are so priceless: "I understand." Put yourself in the place of your teenage son and daughter and try to understand them. Try to understand how difficult it is for your elderly parents to lose control over their health and independence.

Guarding Your Heart in a Tough World

As we live out our lives with Jesus in the real world, our heart becomes vulnerable to hurt, temptation, and spiritual attacks. Proverbs tells us, "Above all else, guard your heart, for it is the wellspring of life" (Proverbs 4:23). As we take up the armor of God in spiritual warfare, the breastplate of righteousness guards, above all, our heart (Ephesians 6:14).

How do we wisely guard our heart? Jesus' advice is helpful here. When giving a prophetic vision of His disciples being sent out into the world, He said, "See, I am sending you out like sheep into the midst of wolves; so be wise as serpents and harmless as doves" (Matthew 10:16, NASB).

What did He mean—"be wise as serpents"? He meant that we are to know the ways of the world, know the traps. We are to understand clearly how people can manipulate, hurt, and abuse if we let them. There are people in this world who want to dominate you and me to perpetuate their own self-serving agenda. One strategy of cults is to demand obedience to a strong leader's personal direction. That strategy is also used by many domineering individuals. Don't allow yourself to be used in ways God has not called you to be used. Be wise about the pressures and temptations that will come your way and know how to escape. Protect your heart.

On the other hand, Jesus said, "Be innocent as a dove,"(NIV). Don't allow your heart to become so protective and distrustful of the wolves in the world that you cut yourself off from everyone. Don't learn the craftiness of the snake so well that you acquire the heart of a snake. In the past I said, many times, "I don't trust anyone." That statement came from a heart that had been hurt by people. While it's true that many people can't be trusted, I took it too far. I became so distrustful of people that I hurt them by my accusations of false motives or unfaithfulness. A dove doesn't hurt others. A dove brings grace and beauty. The dove is the symbol of peace.

Guarding our heart in this world is a difficult yet necessary balance. As one commentator notes, "The caution of the disciples is to consist not in clever diplomatic moves but in the purity of a life that is genuine and wears no masks."[4] This is similar to Paul's statement, "I want you to be wise about what is good, and innocent about what is evil" (Romans 16:19).

I pray for each of us that we never take for granted the health of our spiritual heart because we never know what tomorrow will bring. I recently received a letter from a former student of mine who had gone through some difficult times in her family and in the early years of her marriage. She wrote to say that she was now expecting a baby. She and her husband were absolutely thrilled because this was a gift from God after they had worked so hard to make their lives honoring to Him.

But then I got a letter from her just a couple of days ago telling me that during a routine checkup, in which they would hear the baby's heartbeat for the first time, the doctor couldn't hear anything. An ultrasound concluded that the baby had died. This was a horribly unexpected shock to them both. In her letter to me in which she recounted their experience, she told me,

> Physically, I am doing really well, and emotionally we are healing. The support and love we've felt from our families and friends has been overwhelming and encouraging. We would never choose this circumstance, and pray that I will be able to carry children to term someday, but this experience has knit my husband and me together in a way that good times cannot. Once again, he has proven to be just the husband I need, in ways that I could not even anticipate to ask for. My heart bursts with gratitude for God's grace and generosity in my relationships.

I marvel at those words: "My heart bursts with gratitude for God's grace and generosity." This is a young woman who has gone through some of the most difficult times of her life. What she thought was a gift from God was now a tragedy. How easy it would be for her to harden her heart. Yet she now has come to understand that the circumstances around her must not determine the spiritual health of her heart.

Today is the day to establish a healthy heart. Whatever the condition of your heart, let Jesus love you. Whatever the circumstances you are experiencing, let Jesus' love break through into that heart of yours. Then your heart, too, will overflow with gratitude for God's grace and generosity in every area of your life.

CHAPTER TWELVE

ENCOUNTERING THE TOUGH TIMES

Talk to me about the truth of religion and I'll listen gladly. Talk to me about the duty of religion and I'll listen submissively. But don't come talking to me about the consolations of religion or I shall suspect that you don't understand.

C. S. LEWIS,
A GRIEF OBSERVED (A.D. 1961)[1]

■

Tim and Charlie had no idea what lay ahead on the day they set off for a day's skiing in the California mountains.

They had met at a young married couples Bible study in our church. Both couples, Tim and Becky, and Charlie and Ellen, were in their early thirties and still newlyweds. Both couples were eager to grow as Christians. Tim was rising quickly in the U.S. headquarters of a major Japanese auto maker. Charlie was a professional pilot who loved the thrill of flying.

On the early February day they took off to go snow skiing, we had received more precipitation than normal that year, so the resorts reported excellent conditions. Both Tim and Charlie were exceptional skiers and pushed each other to the maximum of their abilities. At the end of the day, they did not return home. Becky and Ellen alerted authorities, who launched an extensive search of the area where the men were known to have been skiing. Their car was found in the parking lot at the base of the mountain where they had left it that morning.

For the next frantic hours . . . and then days . . . search parties covered and recovered ski trails, wooded hillsides, and open meadows. In the area that Charlie and Tim had been skiing, three major avalanches had rumbled down the mountain that fateful day.

Days stretched into weeks and months. Although the authorities finally called off the official search, family and friends, especially those from their Bible study, continued the search on their own. They hoped that the young men may have sought shelter in one of the many abandoned mines on the mountain.

Finally, as the snow melted with the coming of spring, search parties found their bodies. They had been caught in one of the avalanches and had died almost instantaneously.

Both memorial services were held at our church, and they were incredibly powerful. In each one, person after person came forward to share the impact of these young men on their lives.

Tim's memorial service especially touched me because we had many mutual friends who shared about his life that day. The testimony of his family, his friends, and coworkers was powerful. He was not quite thirty-two, with a baby boy only four months old when Tim's life was snuffed out. But in that short time Tim had begun to sort out what was really important in life. On a business trip to Japan six months before he died, two months before his son was born, Tim jotted down his lifetime goals. Becky found that sheet of paper after he died, and included them on the bulletin passed out at the memorial service. She wanted me to share them with you.

> 8/25/91 On the plane to Tokyo
> Lifetime Goals:
> - Live out my life as a witness and servant of Jesus Christ.
> - Love and serve my family, friends, and the world.
> - Love Becky more every day, and commit myself to helping her experience fullness of life.
> - Raise our children to be servants of Jesus Christ.
> - Live out God's will for my life using the unique gifts that He has given me to further His kingdom.
> - To accomplish these goals and live my life in such a way that it can be said that at the end of my life my years on earth were well-spent and well-lived.

Those final words are almost prophetic: "that at the end of my life my years on earth were well-spent and well-lived." Such indeed was the testimony of family, friends, and fellow workers about both Tim and Charlie's lives.

But the story doesn't end there. Becky and Ellen must carry on. However "well-spent and well-lived" their lives with their husbands, these two young widows face a long corridor of time yet to be lived on this earth.

Their ongoing suffering is undeniable. In a very real display of Christian faith and hope, Becky and Ellen do not grieve as do nonChristians who have no hope (1 Thessalonians 4:13). They live with a settled assurance about the eternal destiny of their husbands. But they *do* grieve. Life was altered forever. Ellen met a young man a couple of years later to whom she is now happily married. Becky and Tim's little son, Joshua, has supplied her many joyous moments. Still, there is an empty place in the hearts of these young women.

The Bible is clear-sighted and plainspoken about life on this fallen planet: We *will* encounter challenges, difficult circumstances, and suffering as we walk with Jesus in the real world. Jesus suffered, and we too may face great difficulties as we pursue our goal of becoming like Him.

False Messages of Joy

I am afraid that many of us have been deceived by messages from well-meaning, but seriously deluded, persons. I mean those who say that if we only have enough faith we will be perpetually healthy and wealthy and happy. We *are* promised an eternal destiny, and we *are* assured that God will supply our needs as we seek first His kingdom, and we *are* exhorted to rejoice always. But this is a far cry from the health and wealth messages that some proclaim.

Equally well-meaning messages about the abundant life have given a false veneer to the Christian life. Life abundant *is* a reality in the presence of Jesus, both here and in the afterlife, but it is an abundance of life that takes us *through* the tough times, not *out* of them.

The result of these kinds of false messages is that most Christians simply are not prepared to encounter difficulties. We have trouble accepting the fact that hardship is a tragic, yet natural, part of life until the Lord returns. We also have trouble knowing how to cope with daily difficulties. Our false understanding of the Christian life has deceived us, and we do not know how to live through the tough times. These tough times can be as monumental as the loss of a loved one or a tragic accident, or they can be as routine as your child being taunted by playmates or difficulty in making the mortgage payment on your home.

On the one hand, many of us are not prepared to answer the question, "*Why*?" Just as important, if not more so, we need to answer the question, "*How*?" That is, "*How do we go on with life and grow when we encounter tough times*?"

Why?

"*Why*?" probes the problem of suffering in this world. It poses the age-old questions behind the suffering of Job in the Old Testament and behind the persecution of the early church. The question "why" stands behind Rabbi Harold Kushner's best-selling account of his son's illness and death, *When Bad Things Happen to Good People*, and shouts from every airline disaster and terrorist bombing.

Professor Thomas Oden advises would-be pastors in their care of those who suffer; he points to the three sides of the perplexing triangle of the question "*Why*":

- God is unsurpassingly good.
- God is incomparably powerful.
- Suffering and evil nonetheless exist.[2]

Why does a good God allow evil to happen to me? Why is there such suffering in this world if God really is good? Is He really in control?

C. S. Lewis is the person who has helped me the most to understand the many dimensions of suffering. In an early book, *The Problem of Pain*, Lewis objectively advanced numerous arguments to show that God's goodness and power are reconcilable with suffering. I regularly recommend this book as a clear answer to the question of "Why?" and have included a summary of his argument in the endnotes.[3] While Lewis' analytical argument can be supplemented,[4] he has given help to millions.

But Lewis had to struggle to find another perspective on suffering. In *A Grief Observed*, written just after his wife, Joy, died of cancer, Lewis ventilated his anguish at watching his wife suffer. He pours out his own suffering in his loss of his beloved wife. It is a journal of his pilgrimage through the land of grief and his attempt to move to the second question, "*How*?" It is in this later book that Lewis helps us also to find realistic help in our own experiences of pain.

How?

How do we live *through* tough times and suffering? I found one paragraph of Lewis's struggle with grief to be puzzling upon first reading. He said:

> Talk to me about the truth of religion and I'll listen gladly. Talk to me about the duty of religion and I'll listen submissively. But don't come talking to me about the consolations of religion or I shall suspect that you don't understand.[5]

Like most of us, Lewis wanted no glib answers, none of the trivial religious platitudes which were offered by others around him with the expectation that he would snap out of his grief once he had heard them.

Lewis had to struggle through the process. He had to ask hard questions, such as the possibility that God was bad and that God was a sort of celestial sadist inflicting pain on His creatures for His own delight. These thoughts were shouts of pain which shocked even Lewis. He had never been one to give vent to his emotions, and now he was almost frightened by them.

But as he journaled his four volumes of grief, a note of peace began to return. The answers he had offered others in *The Problem of Pain* once again returned to sustain him. God is indeed good. Life is not out of control. But now Lewis recognized more fully in his own experience that human life, the full Christian life, includes suffering. He must walk through the valley of the shadow of death.

While he knew better than most the philosophical and biblical truths that would bear him up, Lewis now understood clearly that grief is a reality of life one must experience in the path of discipleship. In one of his last books, *Letters to Malcolm*, Lewis observed that the process of purification in the image of Christ involves suffering. As he looked back over his life he mused, "Most real good that has been done me in this life has involved [pain]."[6]

While we do not understand all the reasons why God has allowed suffering and evil to remain, we do know that others before us have found reasons enough. More importantly, the strength and the personal presence of Jesus they draw upon in their difficulties enabled them to know how to go deeper into the unshakable love, peace, and wisdom about life that comes only from God.

Jesus Encountered Difficulties

One of the clearest issues stressed by the biblical writers is that Jesus suffered, and that we too will be challenged and tested in this life. Jesus' own personal encounters with pain and trial show us how He relied on intimacy with the Father for the strength and encouragement needed to live a life destined for the cross.

From the start, Jesus did not grow up in the lap of luxury. In His day, there were few wealthy people, virtually no middle class, and the majority of the people existed in the lower class. Jesus belonged to the lower class of people. In ancient Israel the masses of people experienced a great deal of daily suffering from the elements of nature, from regular poverty, and from lack of medical care. And so it was that Jesus grew up in a relatively insignificant town called Nazareth, knowing the hardship of a laboring family trying to eke out a living. Even more, He knew the emotional and economic trauma of living as a conquered people under the military rule and heavy taxation of the Roman empire.

In His own family Jesus experienced personal suffering. Quite likely He experienced the death of His legal father, Joseph. He felt the alienation of at least some of His brothers and sisters during His public ministry (Mark 3:21,31-35; 6:4), some of whom did not believe in Him even toward the end of His life (John 7:1-5).

We know that Jesus experienced weariness, hunger, and thirst (John 4:6-7). Drought and famine were widespread in first century Palestine, which severely impacted the common people. He experienced grief as He saw the real needs of real people (Matthew 9:35-38). He cried in deep sorrow at the grave of His friend Lazarus (John 11:33-35).

Then came the Cross.

The Cross was the most intense suffering of Jesus' earthly life. His agonizing prayers in the garden express His dread at the prospect of a tortured death. New Testament scholar Martin Hengel has studied crucifixion in the ancient world, and his discoveries give sobering insights to Jesus' death.[7] But even more importantly, the prospect of separation from the Father was a greater horror.

Once again it may be that we are so familiar with the stories of Jesus' crucifixion that we are numb to the human suffering He experienced. During the period of darkness in His crucifixion, Jesus became the sin offering for humanity. William Hendricksen describes the scene graphically:

> The darkness meant judgment, the judgment of God upon our sins, his wrath as it were burning itself out in the very heart of Jesus, so that He, as our Substitute, suffered most intense agony, indescribable woe, terrible isolation or forsakenness. Hell came to Calvary that day, and the Savior descended into it and bore its horrors in our stead.[8]

Jesus Leads Us through

Jesus taught us many lessons in the way He endured the difficulties and sufferings of life. Among them we see clearly the following:

First, Jesus trusted His life, His spirit, into the Father's hands. Even though it looked like life was out of control, Jesus trusted His very spirit fully to the Father's care. He knew that the Father loved Him and that anything He was called to do was necessary for the greater good of the Father's purposes for humanity.

Second, Jesus obeyed the Father's will for His life, even though it meant suffering. It was not enough simply to know the Father's will, it was necessary to follow through on the work to which He was called. That is why all disciples are called to take up our cross daily. The cross stands as the highest symbol of the Father's will for Jesus' and our lives. As we surrender our own will and allow it to become one with the Father's, we are able to bring the experience of the kingdom of God just a bit closer to those around us.

Third, Jesus called upon the intimacy of His relationship to His Father in the most difficult of His circumstances. In addressing His prayers, both in Gethsemane and on the cross, to *Abba*, Father, Jesus acknowledged the intimate, Father-Son relationship which was at the center of His very existence. A loving Father will never abandon His Son, even though there may be a forced separation. As Jesus cried out His confidence in the security of His relationship with the Father, it was a means of consciously helping us live in the strength of that relationship.

Do you trust your life to the Father's hands? Trust means simply taking God at His word. He has promised to be with you in all circumstances. Do you trust that He is always with you?

When you encounter difficulties, do you continue to remain obedient to God's calling on your life? Or do you try to take back your life and run away when the hard times come? You will quite likely experience some hard times in your marriage. Are you ready to walk out when the difficult times come? Or will you stay obedient to the vows you made to your spouse before God?

When the tough times come, be ready to call out to the Father. Talk to Him, let Him know your frustrations, give vent to your anger or your fear. He loves you as His child, and He understands. He will love you *and* empower you to face your difficulties with renewed confidence and courage.

As we grow in Christ, we can also learn how to open our hearts in each difficulty to receive strength and help from God. Let's now look at some of life's difficulties and the ways in which God consoles us in those difficulties. C. S. Lewis eventually returned to these consolations as he grew deeper in faith. In them he found the comfort and strength to find his way through the most painful experiences of his life. They have comforted people of faith throughout the centuries. The consolations that the Word of God gives us are:

- God is not indifferent.
- God uses suffering for our good.
- Suffering unites us to Christ.
- God is the God of all comfort.
- Suffering will not endure forever.

As we learn how to be consoled we can become skillful shepherds—to use the words of Derek Tidball, "men and women who are able to encourage and console others in their difficulties."[9]

God Is Not Indifferent

Life offers daily challenges. They can come as an endless string of mundane stresses, such as traffic jams, bureaucratic red tape, demanding deadlines, and feeding, bathing, and putting little children to bed . . . and on and on. Such mundane issues challenge us by demanding all of our energy, attention, and godliness in order to stay sane and sanctified!

Of course many challenges are more severe. They can include the financial difficulties of a young family or a retired couple on a fixed income. They can include the stress of a single mom trying to work, play the role of both parents, be active in her children's activities at school and Little League, while trying to have some kind of social relations with other adults. They can include church members trying to weather a split caused by the irreconcilable differences between a pastor and a board. These challenges strike at the very center of our daily life.

We can receive consolation by fixing our hearts on the truth that God is not indifferent. He has Himself experienced, in Christ, the difficulties of everyday life, the daily temptations (Hebrews 4:15), and the depth and anguish of suffering and death (Hebrews 2:9).

As you encounter the difficulties, remind yourself that God is there with you, and He cares. Although you may *feel* as though He is far off, overcome your feelings with the truth that He sympathizes with your weakness and knows how greatly you are tempted to succumb to your difficulties (Hebrews 4:15).

He can, and will, offer help. But the place to begin is with your understanding of God. Is He mean and hateful? Is He so far off that He cannot, or will not, help? The psalmist offers this experience as he turned to God while in the middle of his difficulties:

> I sought the LORD, and He answered me, and delivered me from all my fears. . . .
> This afflicted man cried and the LORD heard him; and saved him out of all his troubles.
> The angel of the LORD encamps around those who fear Him, and rescues them. (Psalm 34:4-7, NASB)

Like David, we can call out to God, and He will free us from our fears and troubles.

God Uses Suffering for Our Good

Failure is a word that Westerners, especially Americans, hate. We want to win, whether it is at sports, politics, theology, or love.

I often feel embarrassed and almost despondent when I preach a sermon that doesn't communicate well, or lacks life, or doesn't move the people to action. I was not adequate for the task at hand, and so in my eyes I have failed.

Failure can also result from sin. When I go into the pulpit or behind the podium for a class lecture with an attitude of cockiness and arrogance, I also fail. I may communicate well, the message may be dynamic, I may have positive responses from the people, but nonetheless I have failed because I have actually quenched the Spirit's operation. God may use the message in spite of me, but I have failed Him in other ways because of my sinful attitude.

Failure can also result from those around us who have either failed or sinned. In those cases it may not be our fault or responsibility, but failure results nonetheless.

The consolation for all kinds of failure is that God uses suffering for our good. Failure will normally result in suffering. It may simply be embarrassment at our lack of adequacy. It may be depression from our inability to sustain a career or maintain friendships. It may be the failure of our company when our partner absconds with funds. It may be the discipline of God in our lives causing us pain so that we will repent of our sin and turn to Him once again for our strength and significance.

Our failure does not mean that God will abandon us or leave us in pain. When we surrender ourselves and our circumstances to God, He will bring good out of failure. God can use my despondency over inadequacy to motivate me to work harder. He can also use failure to redirect my efforts toward my real areas of giftedness, instead of what I had thought were my gifts. (Maybe He doesn't want me to preach!)

God can also use suffering to humble me, turn me away from my sinful actions and attitudes, and turn me to Him. He does not enjoy my suffering, but He wants what is best for me. The discipline He invokes is intended to result in eventual good, even if I do not know in advance what that good may be.

Whatever trial or suffering you are experiencing, don't despair! From the testimony of Joseph (Genesis 50:20) to Paul (Romans 8:28), the confident declaration is that out of struggle, God will ultimately bring something very good.

Suffering Unites Us to Christ

For many of us the word "persecution" brings only images of long ago times and far away places. Yet recent issues of *Christianity Today* chronicle how believers who stand for the Lord Jesus as we enter the third millennium are increasingly facing persecution similar to that experienced in the church's first centuries. Wherever communism, radical Hinduism or Islam, or nationalism is struggling for dominance, there is a new surge of anti-Christian violence and oppression. This has resulted in the arrest and imprisonment of Christians and also their torture and execution.[10]

Torture and execution are far from a possibility in most of our everyday worlds. Yet persecution may become much more familiar to each of us than we expect. The increasing secularization of Western culture does not bode well for us. Christians are discouraged from denouncing practices condemned in Scripture, whether it is obscenity, pornography, or homosexuality. In the name of freedom of religion, many of the normal practices of faith once enjoyed, such as public prayers or even displays of a manger scene at Christmas, have been stripped away. The agenda of much public policy seems more like freedom *from* religion.

It is increasingly likely that our walk with Jesus in this world will involve some kind of suffering for His name. Persecution marked the church from its earliest days, yet it did not dim believers' passion for following Jesus, no matter what the cost. Paul told young Timothy, "all who desire to live godly in Christ Jesus will be persecuted" (2 Timothy 3:12).

When we do suffer for doing the right thing in the name of Jesus, we discover consolation in a suffering that unites us to Christ. A Christian will find a rare fellowship with the Lord when he or she identifies with the suffering the Lord endured, whether in life or in death (Philippians 3:10). The apostle Peter penned a potent word to his readers that I believe will be increasingly relevant for us in the third millennium.

> Dear friends, do not be surprised at the painful trial you are suffering, as though something strange were happening to you. But rejoice that you participate in the sufferings of Christ, so that you may be overjoyed when his glory is revealed. If you are insulted because of the name of Christ, you are blessed, for the Spirit of glory and of God rests on you. . . . If you suffer as a Christian, do not be ashamed, but praise God that you bear that name. For it is time for judgment to begin with the family of God; and if it begins with us, what will the outcome be for those who do not obey the gospel of God? (1 Peter 4:12-17)

For the Christian, suffering is *not* something to be avoided at all costs. Suffering, when it comes, can be a means of deepening our union with Christ, who promises to be united with us in our greatest hour of need.

God Is the God of All Comfort

Perhaps the greatest difficulties we face are to watch our loved ones suffer in illness or watch them die. I have walked through illness with many people in the churches my wife and I have pastored. I have walked through the valley of the shadow of death with colleagues as their loved ones die. The daughter of one of my colleagues had been married just a short time and had recently taken a teaching position when she collapsed and died of a brain hemorrhage at twenty-four. Another dear friend watched his wife's mental health deteriorate into dementia after two of their grandchildren, in separate incidents, fell into swimming pools—one drowning, and the other suffering permanent brain damage.

The most profound consolation we can experience when our loved ones are afflicted is to open our hearts in silence, waiting on God to show Himself to be the God of all comfort. In our pain and anger we may shake our fist toward the heavens. Or we may hunker down in defeat and despair. But for those who have the courage to open their deepest hurt, God will come with the comfort which only He can offer. The apostle Paul calls Him "the Father of compassion and the God of all comfort" (2 Corinthians 1:3).

We must be careful that in our deepest hurt we do not protect ourselves by hardening our heart against God's comfort.

In our first pastorate, my wife and I were close friends with several other young couples. Three of us went through childbirth classes together. Our daughters were born within a month of each other. We had a first birthday party together for those three beautiful little girls. About two months before their second birthday, just prior to Christmas, one of the couples found their daughter dead in her crib. She had been sick and apparently choked and died.

The grief that young couple experienced was traumatic, especially the father. He had not experienced much grief in his life. As a young believer he had not been equipped to handle hardship. We met weekly for breakfast to talk, and I remember the day he said, blankly, "Mike, as I look out at life now, all I can see is darkness. There is no light at all."

The darkness eventually turned to bitterness. His heart changed. He had been one of the most sensitive and caring husbands I knew, but his heart hardened, even toward his wife. They had given birth to their second child, a son, just a week before they lost their daughter, and he found himself hardening his heart also to his son. And he hardened his heart toward God. God was not good if He could allow so much suffering.

No pat answers helped this young man. He was horrified to find himself hardening his heart to everyone he loved. He eventually had to work through the difficult questions about suffering in this world. He had known them before, but now they were not simply theoretical. Suffering was real. It was important for him to address his heart, as well as his head. Bitterness was causing his heart to wither.

Now he had to turn to God in a way that was completely foreign to him. He had to ask for comfort. Late one afternoon we stood together in my living room and he could only cry. Cry and ask his heavenly Father to comfort him. The comfort came. It came from a clearer understanding and the direct ministry of God Himself, and it also came from his friends who had been comforted by God earlier and were now able to give God's comfort to him.

Ultimately, we must fix our hearts on this truth, that if God truly does love us like He says, He is in control of every area of our lives. He loves us, and hurts with us, in each of our circumstances. While we do not understand fully each of these circumstances, our heart will remain spiritually healthy when we allow His love to impact us deeply, as we understand and trust His protection in our lives, as we receive the comfort which only the God of comfort can offer.

Suffering Will Not Endure Forever

Daily challenges can turn into ongoing personal hardships. The man in his late fifties who loses his job because of corporate downsizing faces financial and emotional hardship he never knew existed. The mother in her mid-forties whose cancer was discovered just as her only daughter is leaving junior high is faced with the fear of dying before her daughter is out of high school. The man in his early thirties who develops a crippling disease watches the joys of an active life being snatched away from him.

John Bunyan, the Puritan writer, faced much personal difficulty, including imprisonment for the gospel, ill health, and finally, an untimely death. His perspective on death in *Pilgrim's Progress* is graphically helpful.

In Pilgrim's journey, Death is the final Difficulty. The approach to death is like passing through a river. The Celestial City lies on the far side. There is no other way of gaining access to the city except the river, through which everyone must pass. The instructions given are, "You shall find the river deeper or shallower, as you believe in the King of the Place."

Pilgrim entered the river, but found that the "sorrows of Death" and the "Horror of Mind and Heart-Fears" overwhelmed him. His faith founders in the River of Death until his companion, Hopeful, comes with consolation. He brings Jesus' message of forgiveness of sin and the conquering of death through the Resurrection.

As Pilgrim takes to heart that message, he "found Ground to stand upon, and so it followed, that the rest of the River was but shallow: Thus they got over."[11]

No, the suffering of this life will not endure forever. As we face our own illnesses, and finally the river of death, take to heart those words of instruction: "You shall find the river deeper or shallower, as you believe in the King of the Place."

In the last few years I have watched my wife's mother, Margaret, take to heart that message. She is a strong and independent woman. In her early twenties she was the first woman worker at an aircraft company in Los Angeles during World War II. She was the independent contractor while building their family home when she was in her thirties. In her forties she took her aging father back to their homeland in Norway for the first visit since she had left as a child. She has taken trips, often by herself, all over the world because she loves to travel. In her fifties and sixties she devoted herself to helping her children and their families sustain themselves while training for and being in Christian ministries. She is a rather strong-willed Norwegian who has been the strength behind the family!

About ten years ago she was diagnosed as having multiple sclerosis. We have watched her slowly lose her mobility and strength. She now needs a walker or wheelchair most of the time. In a short while she will be confined to bed. She is in almost perpetual pain as her muscles deteriorate and her bones collapse together. She loses energy after performing even the easiest tasks.

Margaret's unshakable faith in the "King of the Place" sustains her. She is a vibrant Christian. Even though she has almost never been sick during her life, she can talk of her pain. She can lament her lack of strength and the independence she used to have. But she will look you straight in the eye and say with unwavering confidence, "My suffering will not endure forever."

The consolation that sounds so gloomy while we are in the strength of our youth is increasingly realistic as time and experience open our eyes. Time will bring us all to the place where we need to fix our hearts on the truth: Suffering will not endure forever. One of the apostle Paul's most intensely personal statements concerns his own suffering. He writes:

> We do not want you to be uninformed, brothers, about the hardships we suffered in the province of Asia. We were under great pressure, far beyond our ability to endure, so that we despaired even of life. Indeed, in our hearts we felt the sentence of death. But this happened that we might not rely on ourselves but on God, who raises the dead. (2 Corinthians 1:8-9)

Paul was delivered from that particular sentence of death, but he would eventually face it again. The greatest consolation for Paul was that suffering would not endure. Eventually he would be in the loving hands of the One who would raise him from the dead. Death could never consume Him.

Our Example for Others

In all of the difficulties we will encounter while walking with Jesus in the real world, we learn some of the most important lessons of life. And they are not only for us. As we experience God's power, presence, and comfort, we become a source of example and comfort for those who will follow in our footsteps. The apostle Paul blesses the God of all comfort, who, he says,

> comforts us in all our troubles, so that we can comfort those in any trouble with the comfort we ourselves have received from God. For just as the sufferings of Christ flow over into our lives, so also through Christ our comfort overflows. (2 Corinthians 1:4-5)

I watch people. Not to judge them. Not to find my sole hope in them, either. But as I watch people who have set their eyes on Jesus, they become for me the example—however imperfectly—of the way I can live my life with Jesus.

My mother-in-law is an example of approaching the river of death with such faith in the "King of the Place" that the river will barely cover her ankles. I need that example.

The example of my colleagues who have lost loved ones helps me to unwaveringly live the truth of the gospel no matter what the circumstances. When I lost my brother I was given the most comfort and strength by my friend and colleague Bob, who had lost his daughter.

The example of the two young women who lost their husbands in an avalanche shows me how to experience the grief and how to continue to live in the power and joy of the Savior.

You are not alone in your tough times, my friend. As Paul says, "Just as the sufferings of Christ flow over into our lives, so also through Christ our comfort overflows." I have tried to open both the Word of God and the lives of others to you so that you can see how to live through your difficulties. May you find the comfort of Christ, and may you in turn become a source of comfort to others as they see your life transformed by His love.

CHAPTER THIRTEEN

WALKING WITH JESUS IN THE REAL WORLD

The time of business does not with me differ from the time of prayer; and in the noise and clatter of my kitchen, while several persons are at the same time calling for different things, I possess God in as great tranquillity as if I were upon my knees at the blessed sacrament.

BROTHER LAWRENCE,
THE PRACTICE OF THE PRESENCE OF GOD (CIRCA A.D. 1670)[1]

■

Discipleship is walking with Jesus in the real world. And the real world is wherever God has placed you to live—living your life the way He intended it to be lived.

If you have ever gone for a weekend retreat to a Christian conference grounds you may have heard someone say, "When you get down from the mountaintop experience, and into the *real world*, you'll be in for a shock."

Be careful not to draw artificial distinctions between the "Christian world" and the "real world." As we've seen, God encourages us to gather together as Christians to recuperate, recover, encourage each other, celebrate, and to receive training that will equip us to live like Christ wherever God calls us.

Jesus wants to go with you to work as well as to church. He wants to be with you as you parent your children . . . with you on that date to the high school prom . . . with you as you volunteer at the town rummage sale. In the adult class I taught at our church for the last six years, I've watched a remarkable array of people being transformed in the image of Christ in a remarkable array of life's callings. Among them are:

- gardeners
- artists
- farmers
- professors
- medical doctors
- painters
- accountants
- school teachers
- firemen
- homemakers
- city administrators
- construction workers
- waitresses
- engineers
- professional surfers

I can say without any hesitation that each has come to experience a walk with Jesus that is just as real out in the world as it is at church. And so it should be, because Jesus came to make a difference in your walk and mine in this world wherever He leads.

An Ancient Heritage

This theme—"walking with Jesus in the real world"—has a long biblical history and a long heritage in the church.

In Moses' final charge to the people of Israel he said:

> And now, O Israel, what does the LORD your God ask of you but to fear the LORD your God, to walk in all his ways, to serve the LORD your God with all your heart and with all your soul, and to observe the LORD's commands and decrees that I am giving you today for your own good? (Deuteronomy 10:12-13)

King David called out:

> Make me know Thy ways, O LORD; Teach me Thy paths.
> Lead me in Thy truth and teach me, For Thou art the God of my salvation; . . .
> Good and upright is the LORD; Therefore He instructs sinners in the way.
> He leads the humble in justice, And He teaches the humble His way.
> All the paths of the LORD are lovingkindness and truth
> To those who keep His covenant and His testimonies.
> For Thy name's sake, O LORD, Pardon my iniquity, for it is great.
> Who is the man who fears the LORD?

He will instruct him in the way he should choose.
(Psalm 25:4-5,8-12, NASB)

Isaiah declared that God called Israel into a special relationship which guaranteed His presence in every circumstance:

> Fear not, for I have redeemed you; I have summoned you by name; you are mine.
> When you pass through the waters, I will be with you;
> and when you pass through the rivers, they will not sweep over you.
> When you walk through the fire, you will not be burned; the flames will not set you ablaze.
> For I am the LORD, your God, the Holy One of Israel, your Savior. (Isaiah 43:1-3a)

The apostle Paul exhorted the church at Ephesus:

> Therefore be imitators of God, as beloved children, and live in love, as Christ loved us and gave himself up for us, a fragrant offering and sacrifice to God. (Ephesians 5:1-2)

The apostle Peter exhorted his readers:

> For you have been called for this purpose, since Christ also suffered for you, leaving you an example for you to follow in His steps. (1 Peter 2:21)

Throughout church history this theme has been a bulwark of true Christian life. These men and women testify to it:

- Ignatius of Antioch's courage to follow Jesus as a disciple to martyrdom in the second century
- Augustine of Hippo's renunciation of his former life of debauchery to follow Christ, recounted in his *Confessions* in the fifth century
- Teresa of Avila's mystical *Concepts of the Love of God* practiced in serving those around her in the 16th century

- Brother Lawrence's example of mundane kitchen work as *The Practice of the Presence of God* in the 17th century
- Charles Sheldon's challenge to examine each of our daily actions in the light of "What would Jesus do?" early this century in the classic book *In His Steps*

Jesus is alive, risen from the dead, and those who walk with Him on an everyday basis are in touch with life the way God intends us to live it. As a final sendoff, let me suggest some immediate values of walking with Jesus in the real world.

Awareness of the Reality of God

We live in an increasingly secular society which does not encourage, indeed, even discourages, us from having spiritual realities as a central part of our lives.

Fifteen years ago I was asked to give baccalaureate addresses at local high schools because I was a local pastor. I was also asked to lead in prayer at the high school graduations. Today baccalaureate services have been eliminated, and they no longer have prayer during the graduation ceremony.

Walking with Jesus on a daily basis will allow you to have a spiritual aspect to your life that no one can legislate against, that cannot be regulated, no matter how secular our society becomes. I teach my children how to pray in every circumstance, whether it is encouraged by the school or not. God hears them in spite of legal rulings. Jesus is with them even if the teacher doesn't believe in God.

Walking with Jesus in the world in which we live is a practical acknowledgment of the reality of God in the middle of a secular society.

Companionship

Walking with Jesus also provides companionship for people in a culture that is forcing us to become increasingly isolated and lonely. In spite of all of the talk about the information highway and technological communication, people live more and more alone.

This past year in our church we held the funerals of two young people in their late twenties, both of whom had committed suicide.

One of them was a young lady who had jumped from the window of a twenty-seven story building in Los Angeles. This is a young woman who had graduated at the top of her class at the University of Southern California. She had been selected to attend Oxford University on a scholarship as a Rhodes scholar. While at Oxford she had solidified herself as a brilliant young mind. She had only been married two years and had returned to the United States to take up an offer for a promising career.

The note she left behind said only that she had come across something in her life that she couldn't fix.

That is a horrible, tragic picture of loneliness, to come to a major obstacle in life and to face it alone. It is a stark picture of despair, to end life all alone because something was too much for her.

Walking with Jesus provides a moment-by-moment companionship. Jesus promised that He will be with us always, even to the end of the age (Matthew 28:20). And remember that our discipleship includes a community of faith. There are times when emotional despair dulls people so that they can't sense or feel Jesus' presence in their lives. As Jesus' disciples we can reach out to those who are lonely or in despair, offering them companionship and an honest perspective about the troubles of life. Because of Jesus, we have a family of faith that offers hope and support.

Accountability

Walking with Jesus also gives us accountability to be what we say we are. With Jesus at your side you continue growing and becoming what you want to be.

I recently read of a pastor who had struggled with pornography since he was an adolescent. As he entered into Christian ministry he was able to control his problem. Then he was forced to be apart from his wife for two months while she went to take care of her mother who was ill. While his wife was gone, the pastor gave in to the temptation to indulge in pornography again. The result was terrible personal shame and a sense of guilt. He began to question seriously his calling to ministry. How could he lead others if he couldn't control himself, he asked himself?

That pastor allowed his wife to help hold him accountable. Her physical presence helped him to remain true to his convictions. She could be the "conscience of Jesus" where he was weak and unwilling. But when she left, it was as though Jesus left too.

The body of Christ is an essential aid as brothers and sisters help us to stay accountable to our purity of life. But what happens to many of us is that when others are not around, we tend to live as though Jesus also was not around, as though we can hide from Him what we are and what we are doing. To walk with Jesus in this world allows Him to have a conscious part of our every activity and allows Him to hold us accountable to who and what we say we are.

A Real Testimony

One afternoon a young lady from one of my classes came to me, almost in a panic. "Dr. Wilkins, what am I going to do? I was asked to go to the Union Rescue Mission in downtown Los Angeles tonight. And they've asked me to give my testimony!"

"Wonderful!" I exclaimed.

"But you don't understand," she pleaded. "I don't have a testimony. You can talk about how God has turned you around from all your sinfulness, but I can't. I've been a Christian all of my life. I grew up in a Christian home. I've stayed close to the Lord all these years. I've been a good person all along. I went to public high schools, but I never got into all of the stuff that many of my friends did. I don't have anything to say!"

Somehow this young woman had gotten the wrong message!

I sat her down and said, "You have as much of a powerful testimony as I do. Yes, I can give testimony to the power of God that turned my life around from all of the garbage I experienced. But do you think that I want my *daughters* to give that kind of testimony? No! I want them to be able to give the kind of testimony that you can give. You can tell about God's power that was there to help you to stay straight in the middle of all of the temptations and wickedness and danger in our world. You can tell of God's presence and faithfulness in keeping you pure. That's the kind of hope that those people need to hear."

Her eyes lit up brilliantly. "You're right!" she said. Together we worked on what she was going to say.

When she came in to see me the next day, she was ecstatic! As she'd shared with those sad people from skid row, tears flowed down their faces. She said that by the end of her talk there wasn't a dry eye in the place. They even gave her a standing ovation!

Friends, that's the kind of testimony we want to have. I will gladly tell of my conversion. But I want to be able to tell now of God's power and faithfulness in keeping me and my family pure while we walk with God in this dark world. That's the kind of testimony that the world is also dying to hear.

A Purpose for Life

Another everyday value of walking with Jesus is that it gives us a purposeful approach to life. When Jesus is a daily part of our lives, we have a purpose for each activity because we are in tune with God's larger purposes for life, instead of just our own creature comforts.

One of the good things about the sixties was to see young people looking for meaning and purpose in life. They were activists who wanted to make their lives count, who wanted to make a difference with their lives in this world. Eventually that pursuit went bankrupt as the loss of ideals gave way to the narcissism of the seventies, the self-advancement of the eighties, and the complacency of the nineties.

But Jesus has given us a high calling—to join Him in making an eternal difference in this world. Remember those times when you were able to talk to your neighbor when she was having such a hard time with her mother-in-law? You brought hope and wisdom. Remember when the fellow in the next office at work couldn't figure out how he could possibly get his reports done on time? Your experience and help got him motivated and directed to finish the task. What a powerful impact many of you have been able to make in the lives of others around you because you have taken God's calling on your life with eternal seriousness.

Sometimes we help people make short steps. Other times we help people take long strides along the path of life. All it takes is being open to God's leading as He shows us how to make an eternal difference in their lives.

My daughters and I really enjoy listening to music when we drive. One afternoon Wendy and I were driving alone when a familiar song came on. She turned to me and said, "Dad, listen to these words."

It was a song entitled "Show Me the Way," sung by a rock group called Styx. I didn't know anything about the group, but their words hit me heavily. Read them closely.

Every night I say a prayer
In the hopes that there's a heaven.

But every day I'm more confused
As the saints turn into sinners.
All the heroes and legends
I knew as a child
Have fallen to idols of clay.
And I feel this empty place inside
So afraid that I've lost my faith.

Show me the way, show me the way.
Take me tonight to the river
and wash my illusions away.
Please show me the way.

And as I slowly drift to sleep
For a moment dreams are sacred.
I close my eyes and know there's peace
In a world so filled with hatred.
Then I wake up each morning
and turn on the news
To find we've so far to go.
And I keep on hoping for a sign
So afraid, I just won't know . . .

And if I see a light, should I believe?
Tell me how will I know.
Show me the way, show me the way . . . [2]

Do you hear the plea for help?

I don't know anything about the songwriter. I don't know his past or what he had in mind. But he represents one of my primary purposes for being on this earth. I used to listen to that kind of music because I was looking for answers. Now I listen to it because I want to hear the questions of our culture. Now I know the answers. I know the Way that he is looking for. I know the Truth to his questions. I know the Life that he is hoping to find. And I know the Peace that passes understanding that can be his in this world so filled with hatred.

Are we so absorbed with our own activities and comforts that we do not look outward? Are we so isolated in our own mini-world that we *cannot* hear, because we are never in a place to be able to hear? Do we consider the people of this world our enemies? If so, we can never hear their prayers and cries for help. We can never offer to show them the way.

When we consciously walk with Jesus in the real world we do hear, we see, we love, and we give help through Him.

Do you—as an individual, as a family—have values and goals that go beyond being comfortable? Have you trained your children with larger purposes in life than simply pursuing their own pleasures? Have you taught them by your example what it means to be a beacon of hope to a desperate world?

One of the worst things I can imagine is to say, "If only . . . "

- "If only I had been single-minded about my relationship with my wife."
- "If only I had paid my taxes honestly."
- "If only I had been courageous enough to take that career opportunity."
- "If only I had finished my schooling instead of pursuing pleasure."
- "If only I would have taken the chance to talk with my father about the Lord before he died."
- "If only, if only, if only."

My wife and I have made a vow as a couple that we will examine each avenue of life and not take the path that is simply the easiest or the most comfortable. We want to maximize our lives together in this world. We want to know that we have made a difference in this world because we have passed this way with Jesus. We never want to look back at our time on this earth and say, "If only . . . ."

The absolute necessity of living out this vision of life was driven home to me dramatically several years ago.

I received a phone call from my uncle Leon telling me that my father was dying. He asked me to try to come to see him. I took the earliest flight.

When I entered my father's room at the convalescent home in Steamboat Springs, Colorado, I saw a beaten and broken man. He had suffered a stroke several years earlier, but now diabetes was killing him.

Both legs had been amputated near the hips because of gangrene infection. The doctor told me that he had only days to live.

My father had not lived a consistent Christian life. People will tell you that he could be the greatest guy in the world—suave, kind, gentlemanly. Except when he was drinking. Then he was a different man. He could be mean, selfish, and angry. He left my mom when she was six months pregnant with me. I didn't even know about him until I was a teenager, and then I met him for the first time when I was thirty years old. Now it was six years later—the second and last time we would ever be together.

I spent most of that weekend with him. We caught up on our lives as best we could. I found out that he had been married several other times, and that he had several other children.

He told me just before I left that he made peace with God and himself. I remember clearly one thing he said to me. "Son, don't you make the mistakes with your life I've made with mine. You keep on the right path."

It broke my heart to look at this man who is my father by birth. A man with so many gifts and abilities but who wasted so much.

And as I looked closely, I realized that I am no different except for the grace of God. I still have many years ahead of me, should the Lord allow, and the difference between what I am and what I do with my life is dependent upon my consistency in yielding to that grace.

Walking with Jesus in the real world places us in tune with God's larger purposes for life. Not only will we be transformed as we become like Jesus, we will be message-bearers to a waiting world wherever we live and work and play. We can find eternal significance in our occupation that will transform it from simply being a means to earn a living, into our own ministry. We will discover an opportunity in our own families to enter into a discipling partnership with our spouse and to give ourselves to our children to help them become the next generation of Jesus' disciples.

The vision of discipleship we are now seeing is real life lived in relationship with the Savior who came to love us and to enable us to love others. I will pray for you. I will pray that you capture this vision and that you make it your own.

As our lives are transformed more and more to be like Jesus, together we can take this vision into a world that is waiting for us to show them the Way.

NOTES

Preface:

1. The second edition with an afterword to update the scholarly discussion was published with a new title: *Discipleship in the Ancient World and Matthew's Gospel* (Grand Rapids, MI: Baker, 1995).

Chapter One: Becoming Like Jesus

1. Thomas à Kempis, *The Imitation of Christ* (circa 1427; reprint, Chicago, IL: Moody, 1980), p. 23.
2. Michael J. Wilkins, "New Birth." *Dictionary of the Later New Testament and Its Developments* (Downers Grove, IL: InterVarsity, 1997).

Chapter Two: Am I a *True* Disciple?

1. Ignatius of Antioch, "Letter to the Magnesians." x.1; translation from Kirsopp Lake, *The Apostolic Fathers, with an English Translation*, 2 vols. Loeb Classical Library (1912; reprint; Cambridge, MA: Harvard, 1977), p. 207.
2. I have described these elsewhere as models of discipleship. For a complete discussion with bibliographies see Michael J. Wilkins, *Following the Master: A Biblical Theology of Discipleship* (Grand Rapids, MI: Zondervan, 1992), chapter two.

Chapter Three: Take a Good Look at Jesus

1. Malcolm Muggeridge, *Jesus: The Man Who Lives* (New York, NY: Harper & Row, 1975), p. 8.
2. Philip Yancey, *The Jesus I Never Knew* (Grand Rapids, MI: Zondervan, 1995), p. 13.
3. Cited in *The Christian Times Today* (April, 1995).
4. See *Jesus Under Fire: Modern Scholarship Reinvents the*

Historical Jesus, ed. Michael J. Wilkins and J. P. Moreland (Grand Rapids, MI: Zondervan, 1995), pp. 1-6.

5. Thomas à Kempis, *The Imitation of Christ* (circa 1427; reprint, Chicago, IL: Moody, 1980), p. 23.
6. An overview of the theological issues can be found in any standard systematic theology, such as Wayne Grudem, *Systematic Theology: An Introduction to Biblical Doctrine* (Grand Rapids, MI: Zondervan, 1994), esp. pp. 547-553. Some theologians emphasize that Jesus operated exclusively in His humanity during His stay on earth, and that displays of supernatural activity are accounted for through the Spirit's power (Acts 2:22-23; 10:38). Others emphasize that Jesus operated quite frequently in His divine nature while on earth. For example, Wayne Grudem explains,

   > On the one hand, with respect to His human nature, He had limited knowledge (Mark 13:32; Luke 2:52). On the other hand, Jesus clearly knew all things (John 2:25; 16:30; 21:17). Now this is only understandable if Jesus learned things and had limited knowledge with respect to His human nature but was always omniscient with respect to His divine nature, and therefore He was able any time to "call to mind" whatever information would be needed for His ministry. In this way we can understand Jesus' statement concerning the time of His return. . . . The ignorance of the time of His return was true of Jesus' human nature and human consciousness only, for in His divine nature He was certainly omniscient and certainly knew the time when He would return to the earth (Grudem, *Systematic Theology*, p. 561).

7. The Renovarè spiritual formation groups practice five disciplines based upon Jesus' example and several movements in church history: prayer, striving against sin, ministering in the Spirit, teaching and preaching Scripture, and showing compassion. See James Bryan Smith, *A Spiritual Formation Workbook: Small Group Resources for Nurturing Christian Growth* (San Francisco, CA: HarperSanFrancisco, 1991), pp. 13-19.
8. The English translation "deeply moved" expresses a term John usually reserves for anger.

9. Among the emotions that Jesus experienced are affection, anguish, amazement, anger, compassion, distress, fatigue, grief, gladness, indignation, joy, love, peace, sadness, and sympathy. See Dick and Jane Mohline, *Emotional Wholeness: Connecting with the Emotions of Jesus* (Shippensburg, PA: Destiny Image Publishers, 1997).
10. Michael Griffiths, *The Example of Jesus* (Downers Grove, IL: InterVarsity, 1985), pp. 87-103.

Chapter Four: The Real Imitation: The "Nonnegotiables" of Biblical Discipleship

1. Dietrich Bonhoeffer, *The Cost of Discipleship* (1937; revised edition New York, NY: Macmillan, 1959), p. 40.
2. Cyril of Alexandria, *Dialogues on the Holy and Consubstantial Trinity*. In William A. Jurgens, *The Faith of the Early Fathers: A Source-book of Theological and Historical Passages from the Early Church Fathers*, volume 3 (Collegeville, MN: Liturgical Press, 1979). Paragraph 2089, p. 215.
3. Richard J. Foster, *Celebration of Discipline: The Path to Spiritual Growth* (1978; revised edition, San Francisco, CA: Harper & Row, 1988), p. v.
4. Dallas Willard, *The Spirit of the Disciplines: Understanding How God Changes Lives* (San Francisco, CA: Harper & Row, 1988), pp. 156-175.
5. Dallas Willard, "Spiritual Formation in Christ: A Perspective on What It Is and How It Might Be Done," (unpublished remarks prepared for a seminar in conjunction with the inauguration of Richard Mouw as President of Fuller Theological Seminary, October 22, 1993), pp. 7-8.

Chapter Five: A Personal, Costly Relationship with a Seeking Savior

1. St. Augustine of Hippo, *Rudimentary Catechesis*, 4, 8. Selection from *The Faith of the Early Fathers*, selected and translated by William A. Jurgens (Collegeville, MN: Liturgical, 1979), 3:55.
2. See my complete discussion of this passage in *Following the Master: A Biblical Theology of Discipleship* (Grand Rapids, MI: Zondervan, 1992), chapter 11.
3. *The Confessions of Saint Augustine*, trans. Edward B. Pusey (New

York, NY: Macmillan, 1961), [VIII. 12], pp. 129-130 (I have selected and updated Pusey's translation at points).

4. Will Durant, *The Age of Faith*, The Story of Civilization, volume IV (New York, NY: Simon & Schuster, 1950), p. 66.
5. C.S. Lewis, *Mere Christianity* (new ed. New York, NY:Macmillan, 1960), 158.

Chapter Six: A New Identity in Jesus

1. Julian of Norwich, *Revelations of Divine Love*, trans. Oddment College and James Walsh (New York, NY: Paulist, 1978), p. 216.
2. John Trent shows how "flashpoints" in a person's life contribute to understanding one's overall "LifeMap," a most helpful exercise. I first heard him develop this at a family conference where we were the speakers: Mount Hermon Family Camp II, July 14-20, 1996. Thanks John! You are a delightful friend!
3. Jonathan Edwards, *Personal Narrative*.

Chapter Seven: Individual Transformation through the Spirit

1. John Bunyan, "The New Birth," in *Luther to Massillon, 1483-1742* vol. 2 of *20 Centuries of Great Preaching: An Encyclopedia of Preaching*, (Waco, TX: Word, 1971), p. 345. This is Bunyan's last sermon, preached in London, July 1688, one month before his untimely death.
2. John gives special attention to the theme "life": Jesus is the incarnate Word, and "In Him was life, and that life was the light of men" (John 1:4). Jesus is not only the Way and the Truth, but also the *Life* (John 14:6). When we come into relationship with Him we receive eternal life (John 3:15-16, 36; 4:14, 36) which offers abundant life in our present experience (John 10:10). John also carries this theme out explicitly in his first letter: "God has given us eternal life, and this life is in His Son. He who has the Son has life; he who does not have the Son of God does not have life" (1 John 5:11-12).
3. For a good theological overview see Louis Berkhof, *Systematic Theology* (4th ed.; 1939; reprint, Grand Rapids, MI: Eerdmans, 1979), pp. 465-79; or Wayne Grudem, *Systematic Theology: An Introduction to Biblical Doctrine* (Grand Rapids, MI: Zondervan, 1994), pp. 699-708. There are technical theological distinctions in

these different biblical themes, especially when attempting to delineate the sequence of events of salvation *ordo salutis*. While that discussion can be enlightening, here we take a broader point of view and speak generally of the "beginning of new life."

4. C. S. Lewis, *Surprised by Joy* (New York, NY: Harcourt, Brace and World, 1955), p. 237.
5. Brooke Foss Westcott, *The First Epistle of St. John: The Greek Text with Notes* (1883; reprint, Grand Rapids, MI: Eerdmans, 1966), p. 107.
6. I have discussed these fully in *Following the Master: A Biblical Theology of Discipleship* (Grand Rapids, MI: Zondervan, 1992), pp. 228-238.
7. Richard J. Foster, *Celebration of Discipline: The Path to Spiritual Growth* (revised edition San Francisco, CA: HarperSanFrancisco, 1988); Donald S. Whitney, *Spiritual Disciplines for the Christian Life* (Colorado Springs, CO: NavPress, 1990).
8. Grudem, *Systematic Theology*, p. 445.
9. Tertullian, *Apology* 39. 6-7.

Chapter Eight: The Process of Becoming Human

1. St. Irenaeus, *Against Heresies*, 5.3.2.
2. Gordon Fee, *The First Epistle to the Corinthians*, NICNT (Grand Rapids, MI: Eerdmans, 1987), p. 516. When Paul says that man is the image and glory of God and that woman is the glory of man, he is not suggesting that the woman is not also the image and glory of God, or that woman is inferior to man. Rather, he is emphasizing that woman is further related to man as his glory. Paul's point is to correct the tendency in the church to disregard distinctions between the sexes. Humans (men and women) are created in the image of God, so as a species they are the image and glory of God in a way unlike any other creatures; as man and woman they also have uniquely distinct roles in displaying God's glory. See M. R. Gordon, "Glory," *Zondervan Pictorial Encyclopedia of the Bible* (Grand Rapids, MI: Zondervan, 1975), 2:733; and Thomas R. Schreiner, "Head Coverings, Prophecies and the Trinity: 1 Corinthians 11:2-16," *Recovering Biblical Manhood and Womanhood*, ed. John Piper and Wayne Grudem (Wheaton, IL: Crossway, 1991), pp. 124-139.

3. This analogy was suggested by Philip Payne, as cited in Fee, *1 Corinthians*, p. 516, n. 14.
4. The closest analogy is the human parent-child relationship. In Genesis 5:1-3 humanity, male and female, is reemphasized to have been created in the likeness of God (Genesis 5:1-2). Then the author states that Adam, "had a son in his own likeness, in his own image, and he named him Seth" (Genesis 5:3).
5. I follow here the discussion of the "image of God" by Alister E. McGrath, *Christian Theology: An Introduction* (Oxford: Blackwell, 1994), pp. 369-371; Dallas Willard, *The Spirit of the Disciplines* (San Francisco, CA: Harper & Row, 1988), pp. 44-55; Wayne Grudem, *Systematic Theology: An Introduction to Biblical Doctrine* (Grand Rapids, MI: Zondervan, 1994), pp. 442-450; and Millard J. Erickson, *Christian Theology* (Grand Rapids, MI: Baker, 1984), pp. 515-517.
6. John Owen, *The Works of John Owen*, ed. William H. Goold, 16 volumes (reprint, Edinburgh: Banner of Truth Trust, 1967), 3:386.
7. For a full discussion see Peter Toon, *Born Again: A Biblical and Theological Study of Regeneration* (Baker, 1987), esp. pp. 55-61 for an understanding of regeneration in comparison to OT and NT experience.
8. These implications are discussed more fully by Erickson, *Christian Theology*, pp. 514-17.
9. John Bunyan, "The New Birth," reprinted in *20 Centuries of Great Preaching* (Waco, TX: Word, 1971), 2:345.
10. C. S. Lewis, *The Weight of Glory and Other Addresses* (1949; reprint; Grand Rapids, MI: Eerdmans, 1965), pp. 14-15. Lewis uses the Latin Phrase *vere latitat* ("truly hidden") for emphasis.
11. Erickson, *Christian Theology*, pp. 514-515.
12. Erickson, *Christian Theology*, pp. 517.

Chapter Nine: Fully Trained in Communities of Faith

1. Henri J. M. Nouwen, *In the Name of Jesus: Reflections on Christian Leadership* (New York, NY: Crossroad, 1989), p. 41.
2. David W. Gill, *The Opening of the Christian Mind: Taking Every Thought Captive to Christ* (Downers Grove, IL: InterVarsity, 1989), p. 136.

3. Leon Morris, *The Gospel According to Matthew* (Grand Rapids, MI: Eerdmans, 1992), p. 668.
4. Steven L. Nock, *Sociology of the Family* (Englewood Cliffs, NJ: Prentice-Hall, 1987), xi.
5. I am intrigued by the parallel use of the terms for "equipping" in these passages. In Luke 6:40 the term is *katertismenos* from the verb *katartizein.* In Ephesians 4:12 the term is *pros ton katartismon* from the noun *katartismos*, found only here in the NT. The noun is related to the verb, both indicating the process of discipleship.
6. Charles M. Sell, *Family Ministry* (1981; 2nd ed., Grand Rapids, MI: Zondervan, 1995).
7. For a serious attempt to integrate discipleship and parenting see Cameron Lee, "Parenting as Discipleship: A Contextual Motif for Christian Parent Education," *Journal of Psychology and Theology* 19, 3 (Fall 1991) pp. 268-277. A helpful, full treatment of how the church can effectively minister to families is Charles M. Sell, *Family Ministry* (1981; 2nd ed., Grand Rapids, MI: Zondervan, 1995). For an attempt to combine family life and spiritual formation see Ernest Boyer, Jr., *A Way in the World: Family Life as Spiritual Discipline* (SanFrancisco, CA: Harper & Row, 1984); and Dolores R. Leckey, *The Ordinary Way: A Family Spirituality* (New York, NY: Crossroad, 1982). On a very practical, activity-oriented level, see Jerry MacGregor, *The Family Discipleship Handbook* (Elgin, IL: David C. Cook, 1993).

Chapter Ten: Intentional Sojourning in God's World

1. Quoted in Leland Ryken, *Worldly Saints: The Puritans As They Really Were* (Grand Rapids, MI: Zondervan, 1986), p. 35.
2. For a full discussion see Donald Guthrie, *New Testament Theology* (Downers Grove, IL: InterVarsity, 1981), pp. 130-133.
3. Ryken, *Worldly Saints*, p. 23.
4. Cited in Ryken, *Worldly Saints*, p. 35.
5. John Denver "For Baby (For Bobbie)," Cherry Lane Music, CO, (ASCAP), April 11, 1972.
6. For an overview of this passage see Donald A. Carson, *The Gospel According to John* (Grand Rapids, MI: Eerdmans, 1991), pp. 675-681.

7. I have discussed Peter's role in this passage fully elsewhere. See Michael J. Wilkins, *Discipleship in the Ancient World and Matthew's Gospel* (1988; 2nd ed., Grand Rapids, MI: Baker, 1995), pp. 185-198.
8. Wilkins, *Discipleship in the Ancient World and Matthew's Gospel*, pp. 202-203.

Chapter Eleven: When Love Attacks Your Heart

1. Bernard of Clairvaux, "On What is Meant by Conversion and by Rending the Heart," *St. Bernard's Sermons for the Seasons and Principal Festivals of the Year*, trans. Priest of Mount Melleray, 2 vols. (Westminster, MD: Carroll Press, 1950), 2:83.
2. For a helpful discussion of inappropriate fears such as anxiety and worry, see H. Norman Wright, *The Christian Use of Emotional Power* (Old Tappan, NJ: Revell, 1974), pp. 49-74.
3. Cited by Caroline Marshall, "Teresa of Avila," in *Eerdmans' Handbook to the History of Christianity*, Tim Dowley, ed. (Grand Rapids, MI: Eerdmans, 1977), p. 417.
4. Eduard Schweizer, *The Good News According to Matthew*, trans. David E. Green (Atlanta, GA: John Knox, 1975), p. 240.

Chapter Twelve: Encountering the Tough Times

1. C. S. Lewis, *A Grief Observed* (1961; reprint, New York, NY: Bantam, 1963), p. 28.
2. Thomas C. Oden, *Pastoral Theology: Essentials for Ministry* (San Francisco, CA: Harper and Row, 1983), p. 224.
3. C. S. Lewis, *The Problem of Pain* (1957; reprint, New York, NY: Macmillan, 1962). Briefly summarized, Lewis argues in the following way:

   > An all-powerful God has power to do all that is consistent with His nature as God. But it is not a limitation to say that He cannot go contrary to His nature, such as to say a good God could do evil things. Since God has created a world which has certain freedoms fixed within natural laws, He has allowed that freedom to be exerted, even though it is not equally beneficial to all. Fallen free creatures in a fallen world will not be able to sustain goodness.

God's goodness is driven by love for his creatures. Loving goodness exacts the best from the relationship. This is similar to the way in which parents who truly love their child will not permit the child to do what he or she pleases, however destructive or sinful that action might be. True love cares to the extent that it shapes and disciplines and even punishes.

Sin is a pervading evil. Since we are fallen creatures we are fully sinful. Even those acts of sin that we perceive to be superficial are truly a horror to God. God's wrath against sin is a corollary of His goodness. We must understand the badness of sin and God's wrath against it.

The pain we inflict on each other results from our sinfulness, yet God will use it for good. He often speaks most clearly to us through suffering, by shattering the illusion that all is well and we are self-sufficient. Suffering is often a challenge to humanity to surrender to God's goodness.

4. For a brief but broad overview of the problem of evil which pays appropriate homage to the thinking of Lewis while offering a supplementary perspective, see Peter Kreeft and Ronald K. Tacelli, "The Problem of Evil," *Handbook of Christian Apologetics* (Downers Grove, IL: InterVarsity, 1994), pp. 120-146. For an extensive philosophical discussion see Douglas Geivett, *Evil and the Providence of God* (Philadelphia, PA: Temple University Press, 1993).
5. Lewis, *A Grief Observed*, p. 28.
6. C. S. Lewis, *Letters to Malcolm: Chiefly on Prayer* (New York, NY: Harcourt, Brace, Jovanovich, 1973). We can see Lewis balance the questions of "why" and "how" in the advice he offers a correspondent at the very time he was journaling his experience of grief: C. S. Lewis, *Letters to an American Lady* (Grand Rapids, MI: Eerdmans, 1967).
7. Martin Hengel, *Crucifixion in the Ancient World and the Folly of the Message of the Cross*, trans. John Bowden (1976; English Translation; Philadelphia, PA: Fortress, 1977).
8. William Hendricksen, *The Gospel of Matthew*, NTC (Grand Rapids, MI: Baker, 1973), p. 970.
9. These five consolations are prompted by the extremely helpful work of Derek Tidball, *Skillful Shepherds: An Introduction to Pastoral*

Theology (Grand Rapids, MI: Zondervan, 1986), pp. 284-286.

10. Kim A. Lawton, "The Suffering Church," *Christianity Today*, 15 July 1996, 54-61, 64. Also, Susan Bergman, ed., *Martyrs: Contemporary Writers on Modern Lives of Faith* (San Francisco, CA: HarperSanFrancisco, 1996).
11. John Bunyan, *The Pilgrim's Progress: From This World to That Which is To Come* (reprint, Edinburgh: Banner of Truth Trust, 1977), pp. 180-183.

Chapter Thirteen: Walking with Jesus in the Real World

1. Brother Lawrence, *The Practice of the Presence of God* (Philadelphia: Judson, n.d.), p. 26.
2. Dennis DeYoung,"Show Me the Way," Styx, Grand Illusion Music (ASCAP), 1990.

Author

A great deal of real-life experience and years of scholarship are combined in this practical, helpful volume.

An airborne infantryman in Vietnam, MICHAEL J. WILKINS returned to America in late 1969. He attended Biola University (1972-74), and later studied at Talbot Theological Seminary. He received his Doctorate in Philosophy in New Testament from Fuller Theological Seminary.

During his years of study, Wilkins served as senior pastor of two Evangelical Free Churches in southern California. Today, he is Dean of the Faculty at Talbot School of Theology (Biola) where he is also Professor of New Testament Language and Literature. He has written other books including: *Discipleship in the Ancient World and Matthew's Gospel*, and *Following the Master*. He coauthored the book *Jesus Under Fire*, and has edited a book with other New Testament scholars, entitled, *Worship, Theology and Ministry in the Early Church.*

Dr. Wilkins and his wife, Lynne, live in southern California. They have two daughters, Michelle and Wendy.

General Editor

Dallas Willard is a professor in the school of philosophy at the University of Southern California in Los Angeles. He has been at USC since 1965, where he was director of the school of philosophy from 1982 to 1985. He has also taught at the University of Wisconsin (Madison), where he received his Ph.D. in 1964, and has held visiting appointments at UCLA (1969) and the University of Colorado (1984).

His philosophical publications are mainly in the areas of epistemology, the philosophy of mind and of logic, and on the philosophy of Edmund Husserl, including extensive translations of Husserl's early writings from German into English. His *Logic and the Objectivity of Knowledge*, a study on Husserl's early philosophy, appeared in 1984.

Dr. Willard also lectures and publishes in religion. *In Search of Guidance* was published in 1984 (second edition in 1993), and *The Spirit of the Disciplines* was released in 1988.

He is married to Jane Lakes Willard, a marriage and family counselor with offices in Van Nuys and Canoga Park, California. They have two children, John and Rebecca, and live in Chatsworth, California.